HIROSHIMA
FOREVER

HIROSHIMA FOREVER

THE ECOLOGY OF MOURNING

MICHAEL PERLMAN

STATION HILL ARTS
BARRYTOWN LTD.

Published by Barrytown, Ltd., Barrytown, New York 12507 for Station Hill Arts, a project of the Institute for Publishing Arts, Inc., a not-for-profit tax-exempt organization in Barrytown, New York.

Grateful acknowledgment is due to The National Endowment for the Arts, a Federal Agency in Washington, D.C., and to the New York State Council on the Arts for partial financial support of this project.

Distributed by Consortium Book Sales & Distribution, Inc., 1045 Westgate Drive, Saint Paul, Minnesota 55114-1065.

Library of Congress Cataloging-in-Publication Data

Perlman, Michael, 1957-
      Hiroshima forever :   the ecology of mourning / by Michael Perlman.
            p.   cm.
      Includes bibliographical references
      ISBN 1-886449-14-7
      I. Hiroshima-shi (Japan) — History — Bombardment, 1945-
      - Psychological aspects.   I. Title.
D767.25.H6P47   1995
940 . 54'25 — dc20
                                                            95-16610
                                                            CIP

For those in my family
and their love
in the families of others
and their love
not ourselves alone
never human only

The most terrible human capacity is that of profoundly devaluing others who are merely different.
—Ervin Staub, *The Roots of Evil:*
The Origins of Genocide and Other Group Violence

He had to keep repeating to himself, "These are human beings."
—An attendant to the severely wounded
of John Hersey's *Hiroshima*

We pay a heavy price for capitalizing on our animal mobility. The price is the loss of places that can serve as lasting scenes of experience and reflection and memory.
—Edward S. Casey, *Getting Back into Place:*
Toward a Renewed Understanding of the Place-World

CONTENTS

I

HIROSHIMA FOREVER

II

THE MOURNING OF ECOLOGY

Acknowledgments

I cannot mention everyone who contributed to the growth and publication of *Hiroshima Forever*, but I'm deeply grateful to George and Susan Quasha, Chuck Stein, and the rest of the crew at Barrytown Ltd. for their hospitality to and support of my project. And there are friends and colleagues whose insights and suggestions—offered in conversation and after reading parts of the manuscript—contributed more than others can ever know to the shape of this book. Especially (and in no particular order) I think of Michael Adams, Peter Bishop, Robert Bosnak, Edward Casey, Stephan Chenault, Mary Davis, Margaret Gorman, Ethnē Gray, Dick Hathaway, Herbert Mason, Daniel Noel, Gabriel Sigerson, and Merlin Swartz.

My father and his wife, Donald and Cynthia Perlman, and my mother and her husband, Harriet and Gene Hower, not only gave my work and me needed love and thoughtful reflections, but also loans when they too were needed. Amazingly, my father still downplays his editorial skills. And, though I think my sister, Lisa, understands the value of her love, I'm not sure I've gotten across to her how much her critical questions and grasp of writing style have influenced my own.

Nor am I sure I've gotten across to Edward Emery, a reader of extraordinary sensitivity, how deep in this work are the impressions of our conversations on mourning as a form of celebration and hope.

Then there's the natural world—its glorious trees, animals, shadows and lights and rivers and all—reminding me that we have it in us to celebrate that world, to attain a more humane future.

Williamsburg, Massachusetts
April 12, 1995

I

HIROSHIMA FOREVER

1

The Speaking of Hiroshima

It is 8:15 in the morning of August 6, 1945, the time when the atomic bomb explodes over Hiroshima. And it will always be. So says a watch dial on exhibit at the Hiroshima Peace Museum, whose hands are frozen at exactly that moment. The time and place of Hiroshima speak to us all, bespeak the world. Using the language of the first atomic bombing, they tell of humankind's capacity for massive violence; all holocausts echo here. The characters of the language are images and memories, impelling us to think and to hope in words like the following: *Remember Hiroshima. Hiroshima never again.* But the watch's hands remind us of something else: *Hiroshima is forever.* There is no going back to 8:14 AM on August 6, 1945, Hiroshima time.

In spite and because of the irrevocable presence of the first atomic bombing, remembrances of Hiroshima need tending. For, as John Hersey says regarding one of the survivors of the bombing in the 1985 edition of his classic *Hiroshima*: "His memory, like the world's, was getting spotty."[1] In what follows I argue on behalf of the survival of Hiroshima's memory—and call for its purposeful, imaginative cultivation. Then we may more distinctly hear its call to us—a call to sorrow, to mourning, and to peacemaking. A call to humankind's largely untested capacity for sustained collective commitment to *non*violence. In that way the place of Hiroshima could be memorialized in our private and public imaginations—speak to us forever. Or, rather, because its speaking must in any case continue forever, commemorating the imaginative life of Hiroshima can help keep us and our descendants from turning a deaf ear to its wisdom.

The watch dial speaks through the description, on the back cover of its 1985 edition, of *Hiroshima* as a "timeless" document. With the watch in mind, I hope to make plain why and in exactly what ways *Hiroshima* is timeless—or, more exactly, takes place in a "timeless" time—and what that means for the place of that document, and other narratives of the first atomic bombings, in our own time. The watch's frozen hands point simultaneously to the immemorial nature of the first atomic bombings, their still-present effects, and the psychological effects of serious injury in whatever guise. When grave harm is done us, something in us remains forever frozen at the time of injury—the harm can never be fully forgotten or overcome, but must be memorialized and mourned if the psyche as a whole is not to remain stuck in its effects.

When grave harm is done *others*—particularly to one group by another—the unfortunate tendency has been to minimize or ignore the effects of the injury and to focus one's remembering exclusively on one's own pains and achievements. This exclusivity adds to the harm done the others, stifles the freedom of imagination, stunts our moral integrity, and further injures the human spirit by preventing us from mourning the loss suffered by those others. The loss of freedom involved in such loss of mournful regard for those different from ourselves results in political injury as well; it always involves censorship or suppression of knowledge and dissent, is antidemocratic.

The Hiroshima watch in question was supposed to have been loaned to the Smithsonian Institution for its exhibit commemorating the fiftieth anniversary of "The Last Act: The Atomic Bomb and the End of World War II." However, during 1994, veterans' groups and politicians vociferously objected to the content of the exhibit script, claiming that it did a disservice to veterans of World War II by its frank commemoration of the sufferings of atomic bomb victims. They were also upset by its presentation of historians' evidence that the atomic bombings—contrary to the usual story—were not needed to force Japan to surrender unconditionally and forestall an American invasion of Japan itself. They demanded that the exhibit present as fact the entirely unsupported assumption that, as one veteran put it, "The pumpkin dropped on Hiroshima and Nagasaki saved hundreds of thousands of American GIs."[2]

The veterans were offended by accuracy. The prospect of a public display of the true horror of the bombings and the range of historical documentation and questions concerning them evidently posed too great a challenge to many veterans' narratives. We would all have been challenged by an exhibit that presented these narratives not as historically true but as illustrations of historically-noteworthy *experience* (see chapter 2)—and placed them *alongside* the horror, the historical scholarship, and the agonized questions of conscience raised by many—other American veterans included.

Instead, the agonies and questions were denied a place. In a revision of the exhibit script, "scholars [were] forced to recant the truth," to "censor their own historical knowledge."[3] In addition, a number of emotionally striking items that bring home the harm done by nuclear bombs were taken out—including the Hiroshima watch. Then, in January 1995, the exhibit was effectively cancelled: it was announced that only the forward fuselage of the *Enola Gay*—the B-29 that dropped the Hiroshima bomb—would be displayed. The cancellation of the exhibit's spirit came first; then, in a notable irony, all images of Hiroshima's agony were blotted out by the same instrument that had given rise to them.

And yet the watch remains, its hands still frozen where they are, and still pointing to where we have yet to go, to where we must go if we would summon the political courage and imaginative freedom needed to forge a more humane and democratic planetary future. A future in which we live and die embodying Nelson Mandela's insight: "to be free is not merely to cast off one's chains, but to live in a way that respects and enhances the freedom of others."[4] A future in which the timeless time of Hiroshima and Nagasaki is freely granted its place, together with its ecology of mourning.

The ecology of mourning characterizing the spirit of Hiroshima has to do with the capacity for deep and enduring sorrow over the losses suffered by *others* in places and times that are foreign to us. In doing so, we remember as well the complexities and contradictions of strangers—and our own capacities for hospitality and kindness. Imagine, if you will, an exhibit on Hiroshima that includes, along with a historically accurate account of the first atomic bombings and the questions surrounding them, a recounting of the following scene from Hersey's *Hiroshima*. In it, a Japanese woman offers a foreigner—and fellow bomb victim—tea leaves for his thirst, with a "gentleness" that "made [him] . . . want to cry," so great was the contrast with "the hatred of foreigners" he had been experiencing of late.[5] Through such intricate and hospitable forms of commemoration, we can bring home in our imaginations those people, places, and times that are foreign to us—while recognizing that we simultaneously give a place to an otherness which remains other, to that which can never be fully at home, fully familiar. I'll call this more soulful and inclusive way of memory "psychological commemoration." Strange it may be, but exploring psychological commemoration in detail (chapters 3–5) shows how a deeper and more imaginative mournfulness can inspire and shelter a more expansive and imaginative hopefulness.

Hiroshima embodies an *ecology* of mourning in several distinct yet interrelated senses. I mean "ecology" quite literally, in the usual sense of the word—the study of the interrelationships among the beings, powers, and physical things in the natural world. Ecology in this sense also implies *concern* for those beings—and an awareness that they are distinct yet inseparable from the human world. The link to the cultivation of mournful attentiveness to the losses of others is easy enough to establish. For, as Peter Bishop writes, through the symbolic idea of ecology, "concern for images of the *Other* is becoming more important than concern for images of *Self*."[6] Ecology focuses attention on what lies beyond the boundaries of humanly-constructed self and group identities. Not attention alone, but active concern—and, perchance, love. For love also fires ecological concern: love for what is not us.

Ecological concern, moreover, has specific Hiroshima roots. These are apparent in Robert Jay Lifton's exploration of *Death in Life: Survivors of Hiroshima*. Survivors experienced, as he noted, an immediate sense of a world ending—an environmental collapse. Subsequently, rumors emerged to the effect that due to radiation trees, grass, and flowers would never grow again in Hiroshima—fears of "nature . . . drying up altogether . . ."[7] Said one survivor: "Without trees and grass you can't live." Said another, "the A-bomb kills not only people but also trees and grass. . . . This makes me extremely afraid." These fears, together with other effects of radiation poisoning and the actual effects of the bomb on the local natural environment—burned dead trees reminding people of what the bomb did, and the riotous and paradoxical growth of weeds throughout the city in the weeks following the bombing—rendered the disaster in unsettling ecological images. Such images, in fact, provide the final chapter of Hersey's original *Hiroshima* its title, whose double meaning evokes the psychological and physical effects of radiation poisoning: "Panic Grass and Feverfew."

Subsequent more general fear regarding nuclear weapons—their manufacture, testing, and possible detonation in war—has also fertilized the growth of ecological concern. Historian Spencer Weart observes that "nuclear fear," especially fear of radioactive fallout, "took a special place" in the ecological movements that developed during the early to mid-1960s, and infused works such as Rachel Carson's *Silent Spring*.[8] But all ecological concern has some psychological location in the place of the first atomic bombing. Remembering the place of Hiroshima can become a way of acknowledging its ghostly presence in all subsequent ecological dilemmas, including contemporary concerns about deforestation, global climatic upheaval, and effects of commercial and military toxins. We can then recognize in the place of Hiroshima a generative ecological presence—a place inclusive of others, human and nonhuman. A spirit animating all future fear regarding human destructive effects on nature, and all future love of nature.

There is much more to be said about the specific character of the *place* "Hiroshima," of what we learn from it about the ecology of place itself in our lives (see chapters 6, 8, and 12)—especially in a time during which all places are in some way at risk. Hiroshima evokes the felt placelessness in contemporary life, and perhaps, in its depths, the "loss of place" that comes with "our animal mobility," in the words of the epigraph from Edward Casey—a form of uprootedness that has dogged us since before we were human. Hiroshima is, on many levels, a primal place of loss; its ecology is one of mourning. It is the place of inescapable sadness—the root image of a leveled and defoliated world. Hiroshima lays bare the *mourning of ecology,* the way in which ecological awareness arises from a sense of loss—past, present, anticipated.

Fear, guilt, and grief cannot stand alone as motivators for the work of ecological preservation and restoration that presses upon us (though planetary demilitarization, inspired by wise fear and combined with sustained commitment to peace, is crucial to that work). Love, celebration, erotic participation in the world's sensuality, joy, quiet contentment, and many other emotional qualities are just as vital. Yet just those qualities are diminished unless we also allow places for the inescapably sad, for all emotions are vitally linked in the soul's ecology. When we try and evade giving losses their due through mourning, our lives falter. As Brent Staples ruefully cautions us in his recent memoir, *Parallel Time: Growing Up in Black and White,* "The rituals of grief and burial bear the dead away. Cheat those rituals and you risk keeping the dead with you always in forms that you mightn't like. Choose carefully the funerals you miss."[9] And when we think of Hiroshima, many missed funerals are remembered, uncensored.

What is it that we mourn in opening our imaginations to the presence of Hiroshima, of those funerals we often miss? The vast harm and violence human beings have inflicted on each other, on the world. The truth that countless persons have suffered and died in needless, untimely ways as a result of cultures organized around the use of mass violence. That the ecology of the planet itself has suffered vast harm at our hands. This realization goes much deeper than does blame—though rage and anger can arise from it. Nor does it presuppose any particular worldview—though it does, in part through the anger and compassion it can arouse, impel our imaginations to consider possibilities for radical cultural change with new urgency. For it opens us to profound, enduring sorrow.

Yet, where sorrow is, there also is desire. We wish as well as fear to grieve; the work of mourning can be a labor of love.

I'm returning in this book to an earlier preoccupation with memory, war, and the place of Hiroshima.[10] I do so in part because the hopes and opportunities occasioned by the ending of the Cold War have in the past few years been gravely injured by complexly interwoven patterns of historical forgetfulness, censorship, violence; by the politics of short-term thinking, of exclusive self-interest, and of hate; and—especially in the United States—by the rise of virulently anti-environmental politicians, talk-show hosts, and interest groups.

Remember some of the things that happened during 1994: the shell that landed in a marketplace in Sarajevo, slaughtering dozens and wounding hundreds of people; the massacre of dozens of Palestinians during their early morning worship service at the Tomb of the Patriarchs in the Israeli-occupied West Bank town of Hebron; the bombing of a crowded bus in Tel Aviv; the political ascendancy of authoritarian rich people claiming to speak for ordinary folks in the United States; attacks on foreigners in Algeria and Egypt by Muslim extremists, and on workers at American reproductive health clinics by Christian extremists; the political defeats of the American environmental movement; the smuggling of weapons-grade plutonium from the former Soviet Union; and needless episodes of tension between the two nuclear superpowers.

In Rwanda, there was ultimate horror: the death and dismemberment of hundreds of thousands of citizens, tens of thousands of whose bodies subsequently floated down the Kagera River into Lake Victoria. This created an acute ecological crisis in shore districts of Uganda, later repeated in the massive outbreaks of disease among Rwandan refugees camped amidst volcanic rock over the Zairean border. But something in us all, in our fluid possibilities, is fouled by the world's failure to halt such massacres. Where, we must wonder, were the rivers of peace demonstrators, when their waters were most needed?

The world's failure to move rapidly toward nuclear disarmament in the aftermath of the Cold War has also created new openings for planet-wide death and terror. For example, there have been completely unnecessary conflicts in U.S.-Russian relations. 1994 began with a Cold-War like dispute over spying by Russians on Americans spying on Russians, widely reported at the time in the American press. Throughout the year, tensions over how to halt the holocaust in Bosnia, together with a lack of timely and considered conversations about those differences, polluted the two countries' relationship. Ideologies of division took new root as Russians tended toward questionable support of the Bosnian Serbs and American policymakers made the questionable assumption that NATO (the North Atlantic Treaty Organization, originally formed in opposition to the defunct Soviet-led Warsaw Pact) should expand eastward, despite Russian fears of encirclement. 1994 went on to conclude with the disastrous Russian military intervention in Chechnya—and another incident, barely mentioned in the American press, whose irony is illuminated when juxtaposed with the earlier spy story. It involved an arms deal in which the United States surreptitiously purchased a Russian missile-defense system from the state of Belarus, despite Russian objections. This exhibits a basic lack of respect, whose consequences are reflected in the remark of one thoughtful Russian military analyst in the liberal paper *Sivodnia* [Today]: "Such secret operations were customary for the CIA and the KGB during the Cold War. Apparently, Washington's real attitude to Moscow hasn't changed much despite all talks about partnership."[11]

Cold-War ways of thinking and acting, abetted by lack of public attention to planetary concerns and international relations, thus flowered anew as we moved into the year marking the fiftieth anniversaries of the first atomic bombings. And other threats of war and nuclear proliferation have continued to bloom exuberantly, the variegated blossoms of an ignored and deadly garden.

Nuclear anxieties keep haunting me. I think of Robert Lowell's poem, "Fall 1961," which describes "the chafe and jar/of nuclear war . . ."[12] I am abraded, rubbed ever more raw, by the massive violence that has been, that is, that threatens.

Despite the violence, the end of the Cold War and of apartheid remain two of our century's exemplary confirmations that the persistence of citizens working for betterment under the most adverse conditions can bear fruit. Yet, when the attempted Soviet coup of August 1991 collapsed and euphoric citizens gathered in Moscow, we did not demonstrate in solidarity with them. When Nelson Mandela became president of South Africa, we failed to dance in the streets. And we have yet to study and apply to our society the lessons of the South African struggle for freedom.

Our minimal response to these events—and others, such as the movements toward peace in the Middle East and Northern Ireland, which defied ongoing difficulty and undermined realistic expectation—reflects a great failure of policy and imagination in the immediate post-Cold War period. That failure is starkly revealed when we juxtapose the opportunities with the horrors of recent years. Preoccupied with domestic and short-term economic ("realistic") concerns, we took no more time out to celebrate hopeful developments than we did to address planetary dangers.

In sum, we have been letting slip opportunities that almost no one thought would arise—opportunities to restructure international relations along far more peaceful, equitable, and ecologically cooperative lines.

Taking advantage of the initial openness following the Cold War would have meant going to some expense, not only monetary: engaging in humane, coherent, intense, and ecologically oriented collaboration with the former Soviet states, as well as many other countries. It would have meant energetic international cooperation on nuclear and conventional disarmament, faster and more extensive conversion of military industries to peaceful uses, and a halt to the global arms trade. It would have meant large-scale but carefully-designed programs of cultural exchange. It would have meant recognizing and acting on the idea that Russians and others in the former Soviet Union had, even in the immediate aftermath of the Soviet collapse, much to offer us in the way of help; through sharing of experience and worldviews, they could have contributed much to our psychological and spiritual self-understanding.

The condescending attitude implicit in the debate over whether we could afford to "help the Russians" went virtually unrecognized here.[13] But in 1992 and 1993 I traveled in Russia, and witnessed several sharp exchanges that were triggered by well-intentioned but patronizing Americans offering help. Nor were Russians immune from condescending attitudes. I learned something about this sort of interaction from my personal encounters with images from Hiroshima and will have more to say about it later on. But the dilemma posed by our neglect of the Russian-American relationship and of the planet itself is poignantly illustrated by the plea of a Russian biologist for outside help in cleaning up an oil-pipeline spill in northern Russia before the 1995 spring thaw. It is "not the problem of 'fool Russians,'" he says, as if to ward off his own sense of national self-humiliation and his expectation that he might meet condescension from American counterparts; rather, "it's the hard problem of our modern civilization, the problem of our own and unique planet."

But we were so exhausted spiritually that we were unable to think seriously about the future of Russian-American relations or of the planet. Underneath the rhetoric about the defeat of Soviet communism, people on either side of the failed divide shared, though to widely-varying degrees, in experiences of depletion, disarray, confusion, and anxiety. The preoccupation with deteriorating economies was given added force by a sense of emotional and societal inertia. Pundits worried about what we would do now that we no longer had a Cold-War adversary—and, in some Western and post-Soviet policymakers, there was a certain nostalgia for the old days of definitive enemies, a dualistic world. Who would be the next great enemy? people wondered, implicitly positing an unalterable need for enemies in intergroup relations. One answer came in the form of the 1994 mid-term electoral campaigns in the United States, which saw the replacement of the Communist with a new crop of enemies: the liberal, the poor, the "secular," the immigrant, the environmentalist.

Such an image of an unalterable human need for enemies is one of those things often called "realistic," while more pacific images are "idealistic." We forget that to invoke "reality" is always to bespeak a *political* reality—is in effect to make a political statement—and that our images of reality change. There was a time when many considered it "unrealistic" to seek the abolition of slavery, since slavery appeared to be part of human nature. And in 1988 anyone who predicted the imminence of the collapse of the Soviet bloc, the dialogue between Israel and the PLO, and the participation of South Africa's National Party in the dismantling of apartheid would surely have been dismissed as "unrealistic." Because such possibilities were not seriously entertained, there was also no support for articulating coherent policies that could have responded to them. Conversely, the chances for the ethnic savagery of a Bosnia or a Rwanda—and the possibility that the world might *fail* to fashion a humane and coherent way of preventing or halting such violence—were not seriously entertained. Notice that it could have been argued that it was *un*realistic to think the Soviet Union could survive the early 1990s, and idealistic to think that tragedies in the Balkans and elsewhere would *not* occur. The categories of "idealism" and "realism" have failed us—as dualistic concepts tend to do—and have contributed much to our present grief.

I do not think that people inevitably need enemies, and hope in this essay to offer a less cynical and more expansive view of human possibility (and one that allows for more flexible, non-dualistic ways of imagining what is real and what is ideal). That, historically-speaking, groups have usually made enemies of other groups, is evident. That enemy-making is genetically influenced, founded on an inherent tendency toward setting one's group apart from all others, is highly likely, although the capacity to transcend such division probably has equally strong—though rarely discussed and infrequently researched—evolutionary sources. These sources and their historical expression are worthy of remembrance, consideration, and celebration. Do not the streams of South African voters breeching the levees of apartheid, still flowing as they do in our memories, call for such considerate regard?

That enemy-making, together with related forms of group discrimination, is a fundamentally trivial endeavor is not always obvious, though Freud implied as much in speaking of the role of "the narcissism of minor differences" in conflicts between closely-related groups. Psychologist Ervin Staub, summarizing research on people's "tendency to divide the world into 'us' and 'them,'" notes the power of "seemingly trivial information"—such as assumed preferences for one painter over another—in the creation of "ingroups and outgroups and then discriminat[ion] against members of the outgroup."[14] In social-psychological experiments on that subject, it is precisely the triviality of the assumed intergroup difference that is said to demonstrate the strength, if not the inevitability, of "ingroup" biases against one or another "outgroup."

Yet this triviality can also be seen as a reflection of the experimental situation: a focus on the trivial may be conducive to us/them discriminations (in the logical and normative senses), and vice versa. Triviality may, in fact, lay the groundwork for us/them thinking, in that both involve a constriction of focus and imagination. We can take refuge in (relative) trivialities as a way of warding off strangeness, the inchoateness of anxiety, death, and vast emptiness. Though we surely need diversions from such huge actualities, a trivial focus often becomes the occasion not for vacation from, but repression of, larger awareness. An exclusive triviality is an effort at adaptation gone awry, a misplaced attempt to domesticate what is unfamiliar or frightening.

Consider two nuclear images that vividly illuminate the process of trivialization. The first is a scene that takes place just before the bombs go off in the 1983 television film about nuclear holocaust, *The Day After:* a wife, knowing the bombs are about to fall, tries frantically to make the bed. The second is in a newspaper editorial which appeared in August of 1994, arguing that the United State's nuclear weapons labs should focus on maintaining the so-called safety of the nation's current nuclear arsenal rather than on developing new weapons. It criticizes "weapons officials [who] want to keep inventing and refining new devices, as a vintner might blend new wines. But the nation would be better off with stewards, who would just take care that none of the bottles on the rack can be uncorked accidentally or have lost their pop."[15]

Consider the images: making your bed moments before the blasting of your home into small radioactive particles, and a nuclear detonation that goes "pop." In the face of unchained terror, of the specter of what cannot be domesticated, we may want to preoccupy ourselves with neatening the house but it will not help. Analogies to homespun realities serve only to quiet our unease, to effect our emotional and political nonparticipation in affairs outside the home.

We are then rendered more vulnerable to the return of repressed larger anxieties in the form of definable, blameworthy others. Vulnerable, for instance, to preoccupation with stereotyped images of urban street criminals in need of tougher punishment while Oliver North, whose conviction on a felony charge involving violation of the United States Constitution was overturned on a technicality, runs for Congress—and while international criminal networks smuggle nuclear "wine."

Perhaps the human tendency to seek refuge in triviality is also, in part, a genetically influenced form of adaptive striving. This may be partly why it is so often operative in mundane situations (as in the experiments on intergroup difference). But considering the lure of triviality in genetic terms can also lead to premature conceptual closure. We have much more to do by way of describing its manifestations and consequences, exploring the psychological conditions that prompt it and that attenuate it, and disentangling it from related phenomena, such as enemy-making. We need as well to bear in mind something else that seems crucial both in our evolutionary background and, most especially, our era of rapid historical upheaval, change, and displacement: the ever-shifting co-presence of multiple, even contradictory, qualities within individuals' and cultures' psychic lives.[16] Then we can understand the lure of triviality (which itself can take on flexible as well as more rigid forms) as part of a more complex pattern of psychological interactions.

Unmistakably, the immediate post-Cold War aftermath was characterized by something that gives rise to an especially troublesome form of trivial preoccupation: fear of foreigners, or, if not outright fear, at least a sense that foreigners matter little except insofar as they affect group interests. In the United States, xenophobic feeling initially took the form of isolationism—opposition to immigration, even to those seeking political asylum (as with Haitians), and to foreign aid and engagement. The operative duality (in both conservative and progressive political and social thought and commentary) seemed to be domestic versus foreign concerns. Within the United States, clashes between differing ethnic, cultural, and racial groups intensified, expressing what Cornel West identifies as a predictable set of cultural "xenophobias" that include the scapegoating of African Americans, women, homosexuals, Jews, immigrants, and others against whom defined hatred is directed in attempts to alleviate despair, the sense of helplessness, and undefined anguish.[17] The idea of friendship, of friendly collaboration between the strange and familiar, got cancelled out, like Hiroshima.

Dualistic thinking represents a flawed attempt to cope with pain, anxiety, and confusion. Social psychologists note diminished tolerance for "cognitive complexity" during high-anxiety periods and a tendency toward black-and-white thinking when grief or mourning is repressed, while historians and sociologists note that economic deprivation combined with cultural displacement can fuel reactionary violence. We could view post-Cold War anti-foreign feeling in other ways as well—for instance, as reflecting a collective form of post-traumatic stress disorder. Or as the outer manifestation of a post-partum depression which stunted our capacity to celebrate the birth of new possibilities in the world. But whatever we call it, the end of the Cold War confronted us with the specter of all that was lost during that conflict—despite anxious assertions of "victory" by Western leaders.

We struggled with that specter, and the struggle narrowed our imaginations and made it harder for us to take account of how the foreign and domestic are becoming ever closer kin. Hence the frequent refuge over the past few years in the trivialities of petty financial scandals and sensationalized celebrity travails. Many became rightly concerned about how such triviality distracts from important issues such as health care and unemployment. Yet I would argue that even a focus on the latter issues, when unintegrated with long-term and planetary concerns, involves a certain stultifying triviality. (There can also be a "reverse triviality" if one focuses on long-term and larger concerns to the *exclusion* of people's more immediate dilemmas. The need is to sustain connections among the foreign, the familiar, the contradictory. Yet there is little doubt that should Americans experience a series of extremely hot, dry summers such as that of 1988, or a decade of catastrophic flooding in the Midwest, the issue of global warming, *together* with its effects on health care and jobs, would become overwhelmingly salient.) Thus, a sustained focus on reducing the many threats posed by nuclear and other weapons of mass destruction, and on protecting planetary existence from other large-scale ecological threats, became largely untenable politically during the early 1990s—and virtually unmentionable during the 1994 election season.

In early 1995, the planet remained largely invisible. Consider, for instance, the lack of attention—both in the mainstream media and in everyday conversation—to the threat of climatic upheaval (a more precise description of global warming). During the first three months of 1995, we faced strong indications that human-induced heating of the planet was ongoing and had already resulted in significant injury to certain ecosystems. In the background were new studies showing that the sea level is rising; that an increase in ocean temperature is most likely contributing to the decline of zooplankton off the southwestern United States; that increased warmth and wetness were strongly correlated with recent outbreaks of deadly disease in India, western South America, and the south-western United States; and that planetwide warming had resumed in 1994 after a two-year hiatus resulting from particulate matter injected into the upper atmosphere by Mount Pinatubo's 1991 eruption.[18] In the foreground were the extremely mild winter in much of the United States (the second warmest in a century, as it turned out), and the strange storminess and flooding in California and in Western Europe.

Yet we seemed hellbent on avoiding any serious public discussion of these alarming developments. An article on the cause of the unusual winter weather in the United States, for instance, discussed the influence of the Pacific ocean current, El Niño, but failed to even mention the possible contribution of the greenhouse effect. Again, an op-ed article by the administrator of the National Oceanic and Atmospheric Administration that appeared shortly thereafter (two days before the public release of information showing the resumption of global warming) discussed the influence of El Niño at length and called for more research into long-range weather forecasting, adding only this oblique allusion to human-created climatic upheaval: better long-range forecasting might help us grasp "possibilities for human adaptation should drastic long-term climate changes bring alterations of existing natural patterns."

This is reminiscent of the euphemistic language used by civil-defense planners seeking to prepare us to "survive" nuclear holocaust. No mention is made of the possibility of human adaptation to *avoid* or at least attenuate climatic upheaval—of the fact that such dislocation has to do with alterable human activities. Such euphemisms bespeak a scientifically and morally irresponsible sort of fatalism, encouraging "adaptation" to an unacceptable status quo.

There is indeed a parallel between nuclear denial and denial of other threats to the planetary future, between a compliant cynicism and the suppression of the images of Hiroshima. Avoidance of the truths of the past, together with recent and present history, is related to the mainstream forgetfulness of the planetary future. And at the time the studies on global warming were released, that same mainstream was filled to overflowing with reports about the domestic murder trial of a sports star. Such are the ways that we pretend our Romes will never burn, and make the bed we will lie in should everything come to nothing. Forgetting that Hiroshima is forever, we do not count the future's losses; forgetting that mourning is a form of desire, we eclipse the planetary imagination.

There are, of course, are many exceptions to this form of forgetfulness, many outside-the-mainstream contradictions. I write in order to add to the contradictions. But also because, undeniably, the world, in spite of the remarkable opportunities of the immediate post-Cold War era, remains far more violent and dangerous than it would have been had we taken those opportunities to heart.

It is memory that keeps the eclipse of our concern from totality. Consider, for instance, the revelations, also during 1994, of deliberate American exposure of unsuspecting victims to nuclear radiation in Cold War "experiments." This opens many things about our history to question, unsettles usual assumptions justifying the Cold War and nuclear arms race. It has its counterparts in Soviet and Russian behavior during the Cold War. I believe that a collective memorialization, jointly created by Americans and

Russians, of how the Cold War caused each side to victimize its own citizens in the name of "national security," could have greatly aided Russian-American understanding in the immediate aftermath of the Soviet collapse. The memorialization could have involved jointly-operated museum exhibits (drawing, for instance, upon the Hiroshima Peace Museum and the Holocaust Museum in Washington, DC), shared rituals of contrition (for instance, during Russian-American summit meetings), and the creation of new cultural narratives and artistic works that would help move our understandings of the destructive effects of the Cold War beyond blame—of the adversary government, and of one's own.

Such memorialization is still possible. It would quicken our awareness of the human capacity—limited to no particular group—to do great and permanent harm in the name of group interests. It would carry forward the insight of the U.S. Catholic bishops' 1983 pastoral letter on nuclear war, *The Challenge of Peace*: whether one views the destruction of Hiroshima and Nagasaki as necessary or justifiable or not, there remains a necessity "for our country to express profound sorrow over the atomic bombing in 1945."[19] Let us not censor sorrow, as was done in the case of the Smithsonian exhibition; for it is only sorrow—a sorrow that deepens beyond blame, toward an ecology of mourning—that can make possible the repudiation of mass violence.

A thwarted desire to mourn, I would argue, has been reflected in the narrow preoccupations of the immediate post-Cold War era—be these economic or immediate domestic concerns, or a focus on the specialness of one's ethnic, religious, national, or racial group. In the former case, imagination remains confined to the "practical" or utilitarian, what is of economic value. In the latter case, imagination remains confined to the cultivation of what Pakistani scholar Eqbal Amhad aptly calls "ornamented history"—the construction of an idealized vision of a group past that never existed.[20] Amhad is talking about Islamic fundamentalism, but a pointed commentary on the political rhetoric of the 1994 American election season by a man who grew up in the 1930s wryly confirms the broader relevance of Amhad's insight, mocking "politicians' talk of the days when all families were intact and happy, when there was no sex out of wedlock, when taxes were low, when crime was stealing one ripe apple, when all school children added sums in their head and spelled correctly on paper, when no welfare was offered and no welfare was needed, when the doctor came to the house and cured everyone, when neighbor loved neighbor and everyone practiced their religion seven days a week."[21] Narrow economic pragmatism and group-exclusive idealization can, indeed, aid and abet each other; they share an anti-foreign orientation, excluding historical complexity and masking death with sentimentality and cynicism.

I emphasize *thwarted desire* rather than *inability* to mourn, because the desirousness of sorrow may yet ramify, opening into more humane and inclusive combinations of pragmatic and visionary concerns in culture and imagination. To the extent that it does, it will involve imaginative and empathetic remembrances of those in groups other than (as well as together with) those we identify as our own. It will involve remembrances in which Israelis, Palestinians, Russians, Japanese, Americans, Hutus, Tutsis, Bosnian Serbs, Croats and Muslims, South Africans of all backgrounds, and myriad others collaborate. It will involve deepened regard for those not human—a planetary ecology. It will give voice to the speaking of Hiroshima.

2

The Forgetfulness of Group Memory

There is a river called Un-Care that flows at the edge of the Plain of Forgetfulness. Those about to return to this world must drink from this river, says Socrates in Plato's *Republic*.[1] If you do not drink with care, you drink more than you should, and consign to oblivion your memory of what you are about to leave behind. You then forget what was for Plato the Real World, true Being. But, being thirsty for life, it is difficult for you to stop drinking. And if you are one of many, all of whom, anxious for life, are drinking the water of Un-Care, it is that much harder to resist the temptation, to avoid being swept up in mainstream forgetfulness.

Forgetfulness itself is inevitable; memory of anything in particular depends upon it. There are times when forgetfulness is valuable, too, when it arises from a reverent or imaginative memory (see chapter five). For remembering and forgetting are not polar opposites but work together in complicated ways.

But there is a certain kind of forgetfulness that is indeed deadly—in part because it is motivated by a thirst for life. For sometimes the thirst for life, when combined with black-and-white thinking, makes us careless, vulnerable to collective or group forgetfulness of others' worlds. This kind of forgetfulness makes it hard to sustain awareness of wrongs in which one's group has participated, and easy to substitute for such awareness "ornamented history," dressed-up memory. And the ornamentation is likely to consist of wrongs done one's group by outsiders.

Such ornamented remembering is captured in chauvinistic group slogans that evoke wrongs done by other groups in order to justify militarism and aggression. Remember the Maine! Or Pearl Harbor, Munich, Napoleon, Hitler . . . These slogans, together with idealized (and often blatantly falsified) recollections of one's own group's behavior in war, tell of a way of memory which depends upon waters of carelessness—of forgetting, of repression, of inhospitality to the actual ambiguity of past and present events and motives.

The forgetfulness of group memory reflects its location in normal worlds, normal ways of thinking and imagining. Which means in the kind of dualistic or oppositional categories that structure the censorship, segregation, and enmity that bedevil human history. These polarized categories lead to a kind of conceptual make-believe in which the world's rich complexity collapses into one-dimensional pairs of opposites, such as particular versus universal, domestic versus foreign, self versus other, good group versus bad group, my (our) identity versus yours. Each of these terms is construed in an intensely literal way, which gives it the appearance of a metaphysical reality and inhibits more multi-dimensional, metaphoric perspectives on the other.

Ask yourself, for instance: Is the glass half-full or half-empty? The answer is not that it depends on how you choose to see it. You cannot create the reality. Strictly speaking, the glass is almost certainly neither half-full nor half-empty. It may be momentarily both/and, but it is never either/or. However, bearing in mind the ongoing process of evaporation of the liquid in the glass, of the constancy of change, a more accurate assessment is that the amount of liquid in the container is never exactly what we make it out to be. What goes on at the atomic and molecular levels eludes any polarized grid.

What this means at the human level is that complexities and contradictions of existence and motivation, and empathetic appreciation of these complexities, are submerged in currents of Un-Care. Polarized categories do violence to the nuanced world as surely as they misconstrue the amount of liquid in the glass. The result at this level is that the soul hardens and narrows; Serbs, Croats, Muslims, Hindus, Jews, dark-skinned people and light-skinned people, East and West, North and South, familiar and foreign, can no longer get along.

This sort of psychic segregation has a cousin: apartheid. As Nelson Mandela observes, the term apartheid was coined by the South African Nationalists in 1948 as part of their strategy to preserve the imagined "purity of Afrikaner culture"; it was "a new term but an old idea. It literally means 'apartness'"—and imposes exactly that: literalized apartness.[2] Ethnic "cleansing" means basically the same thing. While the term apartheid should not be loosely applied, it does echo discernibly wherever the world gets divvied up into warring camps, regardless of whether weapons used are actual and military, or consist of artificial mental boundaries meant to keep specified others out. Let us therefore speak of *ideologies of apartness* when referring to polarized categories, with their inherent distortions and violence. Ideologies of apartness implicitly or explicitly posit illusory images of purity. More collective violence has been done in the name of (preserving or re-establishing) group purity than for any other reason. And pure images do more violence to psychological intricacy than any others.

The words of a Romanian teacher in 1990—at a time when old animosities between ethnic Romanians and Hungarians were reviving, despite both groups' cooperation in the 1989 revolution that overthrew dictator Nikolai Ceauçescu—illustrate the ubiquitous features of ideologies of apartness in intergroup conflicts. Regarding an ethnic Hungarian who had figured centrally in the recent revolution, the teacher says: "Even I, as open-minded as I am, have limits. The man is nothing but a Hungarian chauvinist. Did you read what he said, 'that for Hungarians under Ceauçescu, Romanian became a language of oppression.' How could Romanian ever be a language of oppression?"[3]

Note carefully those "limits," for they are the same in almost every instance of large-scale group animosities. These are limits that stifle imagination, political self-reflection and criticism, and, above all, accurate remembering of the inevitably ambiguous past of one's own group. They foster authoritarianism, which justifies itself by reducing complex conflicts to simple dualities. One could easily speak here of psychological projection—that is, the Romanian teacher's own unreflective ethnic chauvinism is projected onto his Hungarian counterpart. But such projection (or, as many psychologists prefer, *attribution* of one's qualities to another) presupposes a polarized view of human groups—their division into literal and monolithic opposites.

Ideologies of apartness make it more difficult on all levels—emotional, cognitive, moral—to consider the conundrum of factors fueling an intergroup conflict. In every case, the foreign group's faults are exaggerated and the familiar group's virtues are similarly regarded. Thus, the same psychic structure that undergirded the Romanian teacher's indignation shaped American outrage, in February of 1994, over successful Russian spying on American spying in and around Russian territory. The assumption was that Russian spying is necessarily bad and American spying, even on Russian territory, is necessarily good. (In an ironic twist, however, American and Russian investigators subsequently joined forces to fight Russian organized crime.) Meanwhile, during my travels in Russia, I have heard the opposite (that is, basically the same) view regarding the post-Cold War world—namely, that "their" policies are bad and "we" are again being victimized. In one instance, a man justified continued funding of Russian nuclear weapons laboratories, despite serious safety concerns, because "the United States also has them."

Let us not sing the praises of any spy agency or nuclear military establishment; the spy "scandal" of February 1994 was soon recognized as a monumental triviality. But it does illustrate the interplay between group forgetfulness and ideologies of apartness and, most disturbingly, the ease of relapse into the kinds of Manichean dualisms that underlay the Cold War.[4] So too efforts to expand—rather than replace—NATO, an organization that embodies an ideology of apartness and is arguably as inadequate to the intricacies of the present as was its counterpart, the Warsaw Pact.

The question what leads human beings to construe the world in polarized or oppositional categories has led to much thought and research. Is bipolar categorizing—the basis of ideologies of apartness—innate, or necessary? Or both? Or neither? (Binary or bipolar categorizing overlaps with but should be distinguished from the tendency, already noted, to identify individual or group distinctiveness. The imagination of distinctions, group or individual, does *not* by itself presuppose an ideology of apartness. Group distinctness can also be imagined in flexibly pluralistic or polycentric contexts.) Does it stem, as some anthropologists have suggested, from primal experience of night and day, sleep and wakefulness, human bilateralism, or sexual division, or from the accrued experiences of bodily orientation to places?[5]

Whatever their origins, binary contrasts, by themselves, do no evil. The violence starts when binary contrasts become polarized categories, ideologies of apartness. Then, rather than orienting us in the world, they interpose a network of illusions between ourselves and others, providing a basis for both the extreme forms of forgetful ("pure") group memory we have noted, and more mundane forms of shared self-deception, of black-and-white thinking. Once, in a conversation about race relations I (a Caucasian) had with another (African-American) man, he took a black pen and placed it atop a white piece of paper. Then he drew our attention to my hand and to his and observed: "The pen is black, the paper is white. But we're neither black nor white." I took this as a parable. It applies to issues of race—there are no "blacks" or "whites." Or, at any rate, as Ralph Ellison reminds us, every American citizen, regardless of color, "is also somehow black."

Though our skin comes in different hues, our racial categories are culturally constructed illusions in which we too often come literally to believe.

But the parable also applies to the process of making distinctions in general.[6] Ideologies of apartness (but not binary or literal distinctions in and of themselves) sever us from our surroundings, from our own capacities for finer distinctions such as Ellison's. We impose false choices upon ourselves: the glass must be half-full or half-empty. Fixed categories of identity start to congeal. And then—as in the former Yugoslavia and Rwanda—mass killing can begin.

Ideologies of apartness, with their underlying polarities, do seem related to the tendency, already noted, to seek refuge in dualisms and trivialities as a way of dealing with anxiety-provoking situations and fear of death, or of resisting a desire to mourn.[7] Still, the funerals we have missed return to haunt us. Before we face the funerals that haunt the planet, however, we need to dwell a little longer on what it is that blocks our mourning.

Ideologies of apartness undergird not only ingroup/outgroup categories themselves but what psychiatrist John Mack refers to as "the egoism of victimization," in which a group's memory remains bound to the injustices done by others, and the shadow of the group's actions remains unseen, thus prompting the victimization of still other persons.[8] In this form of memory, individuals, groups and nations take on simultaneously the two roles Albert Camus warns us never to assume: Victim and Executioner. For ideologies of apartness seduce people into believing that one can assume the identity of the (pure) victim without becoming, in some way, an executioner. But kill one does—even if one's victim is only the freedom of one's own imagination. This happens over and over: think again of Rwanda, of Bosnia, of the Middle East. Think of our own backyards—our tendencies to give the sufferings and sacrifices of our groups primacy over all others. And the cancelled-out watch of Hiroshima.

Together with this egoism, there is also a *literalism* of victimization. When we become victims, we are just that: literally victims. In victimizing another, we again become literal: literally treating the other as a victim. Because victimization takes place literally, it is particularly difficult to step back from the experience of victimization and recognize its more metaphoric dimension.

The psychology of the victim/executioner plays a crucial role in the political acting-out of the forgetfulness of group memory. Consider, for example, how Israeli extremists who remember only the Nazi Holocaust but lack empathy for Arab and Palestinian travail could work in virtual tandem with Arab and Palestinian extremists who lack empathy for Jews' fears to unsettle, through violent means, the peace agreement between Israel and the PLO. The months and years leading up to the election of Nelson Mandela as President of South Africa saw related phenomena—more deliberate collaborations in violence between white South African security forces and some members of the Zulu Inkatha Freedom Party which marred the movement toward a democratic South Africa. A profoundly dangerous forgetfulness undergirds all such collaborations in psychological and political repression.

A striking illustration of group forgetfulness in the United States emerged during the Persian Gulf War in 1991, when the sufferings and deaths of hundreds of thousands of Iraqis—soldiers and, especially as the indirect effects of the war took their toll, civilians—were forgotten in the celebration of American military prowess. One needn't have been opposed to the war, as I was, in order to feel sickened by the callous and ostentatious postwar celebrations and parades. That was ornamented history in the making. Even many military people ended up deeply troubled by the slaughter of retreating Iraqi troops. And, though the pundits (harking back to the need for group purity) called it a "clean" war for "our" side, persistent psychological and physical illnesses have since surfaced in many American Gulf War veterans. In some way, these veterans have carried the burden of societal forgetfulness and of displaced, unattended, collective feelings of unease, and this has added to their physical problems. Vietnam veterans, and before them, "veterans" of atomic testing, have been similarly forgotten—relegated to the realm of foreigners, of the unfamiliar.

This forgetting of the multitudes of others, this flowing in collective currents of Un-Care and immersion in whitewaters of trivia, is a major psychological ingredient in preparations for mass violence. And the forgetfulness of group memory also takes more ordinary forms, shaping the smaller competitions between human groups for the status of victimhood—the rhetoric of ethnic and other particularity and difference, of grief over more ordinary yet corrosive experiences of discrimination and insult suffered by minorities of many kinds in the world. The victimization is often all too actual; the cumulative injury wrought by the daily "chafe and jar" (to appropriate Lowell's image of nuclear war) of racial, sexual, and other forms of insult and discrimination is hugely underappreciated and usually forgotten by more fortunate or comfortable majorities. The identity of the victim is something more—a literalized image positing an Us and a Them, and a confinement of imaginative focus to the sphere of one's own pure and victimized group.

In the guise of "identity politics," this form of imaginative confinement was perpetuated by many progressive political groups in the United States and elsewhere during years of opportunity presented by the waning and end of the Cold War. This is precisely where the American intellectual left has badly failed us over the past decade; its blinkered focus on domestic group issues contributed crucially to a lack of innovative attention to foreign policy. That field was therefore left to unimaginative neo-Cold Warriors and isolationists. (Ironically, the parochial preoccupations that characterize identity politics make for bad domestic policy as well. As political scientist Jean Bethke Elshtain shows, they vitiate democracy's political imagination, its hospitality which provides a place for the most various people to work together for the sake of all.)[9] A narrow focus on group-centered identity places "immediate" group concerns before all others—and this eclipses the planet. In other words, this form of forgetfulness of group memory, of egoism of victimization, places the entire world on the opposite side of the River of Un-Care.

The egoism (and literalism) of victimization is also strikingly apparent in national war memorials and monuments, where members of one's own national group—and no others—are commemorated. The danger is not in the memorializing of a given nation's war dead *per se,* which can serve important psychological, cultural, social and even religious functions, but in the concurrent forgetting-to-care deeply about the sufferings and dyings of those in other groups. For instance, in the U.S., the Vietnam War Memorial in Washington D.C. powerfully evokes the memory of Americans who died in the war. The sufferings of the Vietnamese are conspicuously forgotten. Nor are there any memorials commemorating the approximately twenty million Soviets who died in World War II in countries outside the former Soviet Union. More recently, militant Serbs have invoked Serbian defeat at the hands of the Ottoman Turks at Kosovo during the fourteenth century as well as victimization by Croats and Nazis during the Second World War, but have little to say about the genocide in Cambodia during the 1970s—or, for that matter, about the Armenian genocide perpetrated by Turks in the 1910's. And Turkey, meanwhile, still refuses to admit that the Armenian genocide took place.

The cancellation of the Smithsonian's exhibit on the atomic bombings is another in what seems a ceaseless parade of attempts to keep group memory pure. There is, furthermore, an ironic and fearful symmetry between the Smithsonian controversy and one that arose at the Hiroshima Peace Museum in 1994. In Japan, the conflict began when acknowledgments of Japanese atrocities leading up to and during the Pacific War were included in the Peace Museum. Even while Japanese society as a whole has become increasingly open to a more accurate historical accounting of their country's cruelties in that war, powerful veterans' groups and right-wing organizations oppose such open accounting. Thus, the Peace Museum's acknowledgments of Japanese cruelty were muted to prevent an outcry by Japanese rightists, while some political leaders were moved to deny Japanese responsibility for the war altogether.

The place of Hiroshima includes us all within its bounds; yet it is difficult to remain true to its spirit. Some Americans have attempted to keep the memory of Hiroshima from the public by focusing on the emblematic *Enola Gay* and the associated rhetoric of American military and technological achievement. Some Japanese have utilized the memory of Hiroshima itself to screen out awareness of their country's wartime cruelties. Japanese and American rightists would seem to be on opposite sides. Yet what stands out is the basic sameness of their positions on wartime memory and commemoration. Each constituency seeks to assert its purity and its victimhood, opposes any societal self-questioning, is deeply offended by the commemoration of outsiders and their suffering—and wields an undue amount of political influence. Even as the inclusive boundaries of Hiroshima subvert all ingroup/ outgroup oppositions, militant groups in the United States, Japan, and elsewhere collaborate unwittingly in efforts to undo the subversion and to sustain the forgetfulness of group memory.

3

Psychological Commemoration: Housing the World

In her book, *The Art of Memory*, Frances Yates describes a method of imagining used by classical speakers to remember their subjects in proper sequence as they spoke. The art of memory proceeds according to specific "rules" for the formation of remembered places in the imagination, such as the distinct features and rooms of a house. In these places mnemonic images are envisaged that remind one of associated information through their "striking and unusual, . . . beautiful or hideous, comic or obscene" character.[1] The practitioner of the art of memory evokes, and moves among, precisely defined, strange or unusual, "emotionally striking" images—images which in their turn move memory. There are affinities, as James Hillman notes, between the art of memory and contemporary efforts in psychology to cultivate awareness of myth- and image-making qualities of the soul or psyche, which require our hospitality to the strange and the wounded.[2]

The art of memory depends upon the intimate relationship between memory and imagination. Memory and imagination are not identical, but usually overlap: when I remember something, some kind of image (not necessarily a visual or even conscious one) is called forth. Imagination, conversely, usually embodies some form of memory (again, not necessarily or entirely visual or conscious). Memory and imagination energize and shape each other. The art of memory concentrates on this co-presence of memory and imagination in the psyche, engaging and making present those images which most deeply stir and "impress" the memory. It nurtures an appreciation of the importance of particulars—particular locations and images.

The basic themes of the art of memory, including an acute sense of the impressive power of images, crop up in many places and times. Traditional topographies of myth, though not less dependent humanly-built environments than the classical *ars memorativa*, have similar features, and oral storytellers likewise move amidst particular locations and "emotionally striking" figures. In Australia, members of some aboriginal communities ritually visit or recount particular features of the natural world that were formed by ancestral or divine beings as they walked about during the "dreamtime," the time of origins. In Old Stone Age caves, there are chambers "filled with invocative and propitiatory images of animals and humans," and similar images have been found in the American Southwest, in an Anasazi cliff house (dating from the thirteenth century).[3] And the faces—human, animal, and spirit—that adorn traditional crest poles at the entrances to dwellings of the Kwakiutl and other Pacific Northwest coastal tribes are strikingly, sometimes uncannily and sometimes comically, memorable. So too the animals, divinities, gargoyles, and Leaf People on building façades from New York City to Bangkok.

One can also find echoes of an art of memory, of "dreamtime" memory, in the growing attention given by ecological thought to the particularities of ecosystems or "bioregions" in which human communities are located, as well as in a growing body of philosophical and geographical scholarship that explores how specific physical places prompt particular forms of memory. It is important to consider that no art of memory is possible apart from an ecological context of some kind. Our location is never exclusively human.

Drawing upon the art of memory, we can cultivate an imaginative remembering of the "dreamtime" of Hiroshima and the spirits evoked by the nuclear age's time of origins, recollecting images that, however contemporary or close at hand, inhabit the land on the far side of the Plain of Forgetfulness, beyond currents of Un-Care. We must then house these images with extra care—they disclose not only the dangers of our time but also that sorrow beyond blame which bares depths of soul. In this way, the place of Hiroshima is given a place in our memories, and we become able to hear its spirits speak to the world's present and future as they evoke a past that—like the art of memory itself—asks both for accurate historical accounting and an attunement to the innovations and riches of the metaphoric imagination. In other words, for soulful remembering, for *psychological commemoration.*

The root meaning of commemoration generally is "an *intensified remembering,*"[4] which phrase nicely characterizes the practice of the art of memory. Psychological commemoration can sometimes involve specific, purposeful meditative or contemplative practices based on that art; it always consists in the intensification of those aspects of memory which carry impressions of the particularities of imagination, and seeks to give those particularities, with all their metaphoric power and richness, the place in our lives that is rightly theirs.

In one sense, psychological commemoration can take place spontaneously—and does so in each of our lives. Consider, for instance, the process of close reading, in which you allow the locations and characters of a narrative to impress your memory deeply enough that they go on working in your psyche long afterward. Think of those characters, scenes, and places that stay with you for life: they have a place within you and emerge at times to offer their perspective on your experience. They remain different from you, remain *other*—and yet their presence brings with it a compelling intimacy, a haunting familiarity. They are housed within your experience and lend it their own wealth, even if they only occasionally appear at the door. For they have been memorialized—have participated in what Edward Casey calls "intrapsychic memorialization," the commemoration of the soul, of the world's interior and imaginative ecology.

Psychological commemoration can also borrow more explicitly from the art of memory, taking the form of more deliberate and direct encounters with powerful images. These involve carefully envisaging particulars of the images and their placings and interrelationships, while remaining mindful that the images and memories refer also to common or archetypal patterns of psychological life—its larger, more impersonal dimensions. Whatever form it takes, psychological commemoration can help us establish a place between the literalized dichotomy of particular and universal. In this, we glimpse its potential to inspire alternatives to ideologies of apartness and help us discover new forms of particularity that don't presuppose exclusion of others, of the varieties of foreignness.

For there is a revealing contrast between psychological commemoration and the commemorating of the war dead noted and criticized earlier. Psychological commemoration aims to quicken and intensity remembrances of those *outside* of the particular (e.g., national) group with which one most immediately identifies. Again, the analogy with close reading comes to mind: psychological commemoration draws on the potent intimacies of one's biographical life while giving place within that life to images or psychological presences arising from very different, and perhaps distant, worlds. It involves cultivating an imagination that is intensely, enduringly, hospitable to strangers.

In cultivating such hospitality, we thus become more aware that, though we as individuals remain the carriers of imagination and memory, they—and we—are not individual alone. Maurice Halbwachs, a French sociologist, asserts that individual memory has a collective dimension arising from the social interactions that begin at birth. This holds true even when one is remembering by oneself: "Our memories remain collective, . . . and are recalled to us through others even though only we were participants in the events or saw the things concerned. In reality, we are never alone. Other men need not be physically present, since *we always carry with us and in us a number of distinct persons.*"[5] These "distinct persons" embody people whom we know and the psychological qualities of our relationships with them—and others whom we don't personally know.

They are also, like the characters of art and literature, persons in their own right—people of the psyche's dreamtimes. Earlier I wrote that ecological concern directs our attention—"and, perchance, love"—beyond human boundaries. But it was not entirely "I" who chose the phrasing. It was also the presence in me of Phil, a friend I've known since the seventh grade, who sometimes uses the word "perchance" to emphasize the point he wants to make. I can hear him speaking through my words; our history together helps shape what I say here. In a small way, as I wrote, I found myself commemorating that history and our friendship. And, perchance, something else—friendship itself. Friendship as its own person. In my dreams, Phil on occasion appears—Phil, whose name bears in itself *philos*, Greek for friendship and love. He seems not only to remind me of my actual friend Phil but of the importance of Friendship. Perhaps I am both reminded to give more attention to friends and invited to commemorate, to the extent that I am able, the daimonic Power, Friendship. Without the presence of Friendship, our efforts to lessen the violence in the world suffer. We are more inspired when we act in the spirit of reverence for Friendship.

This might mean making friendships with some sad, strange images. For psychological commemoration also involves a deep forgetting of conventional views on what sorts of images are acceptable and valuable, and which are not. And friendship means allowing others their strangeness, being faithful to what in them remains completely foreign to our usual lives.

In a way parallel to its provision of meeting-places for history, metaphor, the familiar, and the foreign, psychological commemoration provides for movement between, and the simultaneous presence of, the literal and metaphoric; neither need cancel out the other. For example, the "rules" of the art of memory can be taken quite, but not only, literally with regard to images connected with Hiroshima and contemporary dilemmas. The literal placing of such images in memory becomes at the same time a metaphor for our acknowledgment of the place these images claim in our psychic lives. The literal is itself seen in metaphoric perspective—but the way toward the metaphoric passes through quite literal terrain. This helps us see the distinction between literal applications, which need not be exclusively literal, and ideologies of apartness, which exclude all but one literal meaning of an image or experience, and allow for only one mode of response to it. Psychological commemoration helps us to combine gentleness with precision as we feel out the ongoing interplay of distinctions, literal and metaphoric—helps us to explore ways of making love not war with the world.

The love of world locates itself in *the imagination of place;* so too psychological commemoration. Images of place have their own compelling power—a power that can cut across literalized political, ethnic, national, or religious place-boundaries. For this reason such images call for our closest attention. A place is delimited by its particularities: its situating, orienting, differentiating and habitating qualities that distinguish it from other places. There is, moreover, a particular kinship between place and memory; in the art of memory, each arouses and shapes the other. Place and memory are in continual interplay. In love, let's say. Place and memory, *because* they are distinct from each other, are interdependent, have an ecosystemic eros. This is reflected in the "rules" for places in the art of memory, but the intimate attachment of place and memory may also express itself quite spontaneously.

This happened in the case of Brent Staples, who tells about his variant of the art of memory after relating that the funeral he missed was that of his murdered brother, Blake. His memoir opens with a photographic image—that of Blake lying dead on the autopsy table.[6] Staples describes, with novelistic detail, his brother's gunshot wounds and the extensive and unsuccessful surgery that followed. He carefully and evocatively remembers his brother's physical form; "I know his contours well. I bathed and diapered him when he was a baby and studied his features as he grew." His description of the setting is also precise—poised by Blake's head, for instance, is "a tall arched spigot that, with tap handles mimicking wings, easily suggests a swan in mourning." Staples is viewing the photographs of his brother three years after his death, when he confronts the failure of his struggle not to mourn Blake at the actual time of his death. (For "I had already mourned Blake and buried him and was determined not to suffer his death a second time." Brent's brother had shot a man in a quarrel over drugs and Brent had reason to fear the man would take revenge. He'd urged his brother to leave the area, to no avail.) When he finally saw the photographs of his brother dead on the autopsy table, his capacity to mourn caught up with him; "The floor gave way, and I fell down and down for miles."

This sense of falling may link with Brent's sense of "Living in Motion," as he titles the following chapter: his sense of constant displacement, of himself as "never where I was" but always partly in the future and partly in the past. He was, as a boy, obsessed with "losing memories"—a "fixation" that came, he says, from his family's habit of "mov[ing] all the time." In order to counteract this loss of place—and, perhaps, to mourn what was lost—Brent developed an art of memory. In his words:

> Writers have said that children live in an endless present with little thought for what has passed or what will be. Mine was a different childhood. I paid endless dues for sorrows that were yet to come [as later, with Blake]. I was also morbidly vigilant about the past. Not the past of a year ago or even the previous day, but the past of the last few seconds. I handled memories over and over again, hoping to give them permanence.
>
> This vigilance came on me in seizures that could strike me anywhere: while I lay in the grass making out figures in the clouds, as I pushed a shopping cart down the supermarket aisles, and especially while I stood at the crosswalk waiting for the light to change. I clung to every detail of

the hot rod that had just roared by: the glint of the sun flowing over its body, the thunder of the engine, the twin puffs of smoke from its dual exhausts. I included the backdrop, too: the steepled church across the street, the sign out front that described the sermon and gave the minister's name; the wrought-iron fence around them. This took concentration; it excluded everything except drawing breath. The sign changed from DON'T WALK to WALK to DON'T WALK again. Someone called out "Hey, you, wake up!" and I did. To them I was a silly boy asleep at the crosswalk. For me this was serious business: I had saved a part of my life that would otherwise have been lost.

We'll find that the methodical practice that Frances Yates describes in *The Art of Memory,* though set in classical Rome, is, in both its literal particulars and its spirit, strikingly similar to Brent Staples's own. And there are echoes in each of our lives. Remember, for instance, significant ("powerful") places you have been or lived in (or otherwise encounter in imagination, e.g., in dream, literature, painting): these places are *structuring powers* both constituting and transcending your personal life. By being placed, our lives, like Staples's, are "saved"—suffused though they are with the sense of what is beyond salvation.

Place, moreover, is a thoroughly ecological image, and one that is never fully (though usually partly) human. Psychological commemoration, by intensifying our appreciation of the world's imaginative impressions, can help sensitize us to bioregional powers—powers that can indirectly help subvert our tendencies to make oversimple discriminations or to impose ideological grids that inevitably do violence to the particular features and changes characteristic of a given place.

The ecology of place has political implications. Consider the continued broad appeal of authoritarian political ideologies and figures, even when they have been unambiguously linked with massive violence. Group forgetfulness has an intimidating tenacity.

Yet, the attention to place and concern for historical knowledge and imaginative intricacy that characterize psychological commemoration can directly and indirectly help undermine the forgetfulness of group memory and its ornamented histories, prompting us toward recollection of "what is shameful, base and cruel in [one's] people's past"—together with the remembering of the destructiveness of which each of us is capable.[7] Such complexly-shadowed commemoration helps us resist manipulation by the nation-state or other authoritarian and chauvinistic appeals. (Moreover, politicians who are relatively more open to this darker current of memory will be less likely to make such appeals.) As political psychologists John Broughton and Marta Zahayevich say, "Memory is the place where the psychological and political intersect"; and this place of memory is the place where the politics of reality, or *realpolitik,* deepens into a politics of soul, a careful attention to nonego and transnational realities, a recognition of the place(s) of outsiders.

In its mindfulness of the power politics implicated in idealized images of a group's past (ornamented histories usually have high propaganda value) and in its encouragement of a kind of quiet conversation among many characters, psychological commemoration is a democratic practice. The possibilities of more inclusive memory are apparent, for instance, in recent American efforts to take account of victims of El Salvadoran death squads secretly supported by U.S. officials during the Cold War in the name of "national security"; in Russians' confrontation of the devastations—ecological and moral—of the Soviet era; in French self-confrontation of active collaboration with Nazis during the occupation; and in Israeli anguish over Jewish anti-Arab violence. True psychological commemoration, with its democratic spirit, can take place only if a place is set aside for the sorrowful remembrance of the victims of one's group's cruelty.

Notice that Forgetfulness is not absent here either; there is in psychological commemoration a letting-go, a forgetting of parochial (individual and/or collective) ego-concerns, illusory ornamentations and false unities. The forgetfulness within this deepening of memory also implies a broadening imagination of victimization that forgoes its egoism (including the reverse egoism of excessive and literalized guilt, with its focus only on what I or we have done), and opens toward larger realities of destructiveness, suffering and death, starting with a greater depth of compassion and empathy for the sufferings and deaths of those in groups other than one's own. When we recognize that forgetfulness is not the dark opposite of memory, we can begin to distinguish various forms of forgetfulness and their possible values. The "cure" for the forgetfulness of group memory lies in the cultivation of more humane forms of forgetting.

Imagine, for instance, a day of planetwide commemoration, which, prompted by a deepened acknowledgment of the timeless claim of Hiroshima on each of us, would require humane forgetting of ordinary group divisiveness. A day when the Vietnamese who suffered and died in the Vietnam War would be memorialized together with Americans in Washington, DC. When the sufferings of Palestinians would be noted in Holocaust memorials, and the sufferings of Bosnian Muslims, together with that of Serbs and Croats, would be commemorated in every Slavic country. When tales of the dismembered citizens of Rwanda would be given careful attention wherever there is ethnic divisiveness. When, everywhere, the focus would be on pained and marginalized others. And, also everywhere, on the future of us all, including all nonhuman denizens.

Now imagine something more specific: you are in some place—any place that occurs to you—and before you is some kind of hard surface on which you can write. Choose a writing implement, and write—slowly, carefully, bearing down hard—"Psychological Commemoration." You might want to repeat it. For this illustrates how, in a practical sense, the work of psychological commemoration begins—with impressions of imagination bearing down on memory.

The image you have called forth is more intricate than it seems. It is visual—you see it in your mind—but, at the same time, you have a distinct tactile or bodily impression of bearing down hard on the writing surface. Since the writing is imagined and not actual, it required no overt bodily movements. Yet your body was fully engaged as you brought its imagined and remembered weight to bear in the effort of writing. You can remember this distinctly; the image is kinaesthetically embodied. Also, you may have heard some sound associated with the writing (depending on the type of writing implement and surface). Other sense impressions may be present as well. The image is then a synaesthetic one, involving visual, tactile, aural, and other impressions. You may also sense some kind of emotional atmosphere, and be reminded of other things—things that actually happened to you in waking life, or that you dreamt or heard or read about. For, as Freud taught us, an image is laden with memories.

And there is still more to the image. Place yourself in it. Where are you? Look around, and the characteristics of the particular place (and perhaps its emotional tonality) coalesce. Are you inside or outside (or somewhere in between)? Is it a familiar place? If so, how familiar? Has anyone else been there? Is it an actual place to which you have (or have not) been, or is it a fictive place (to which you have or have not been)? It is, perhaps, a combination of the actual and fictive. In any case, it may remind you of still other places.

Notice that nothing has yet been said about the writing implement and surface that you used. What are they? Did you use paper, or carve out "Psychological Commemoration" in wood or stone? Is the phrase printed or in cursive writing? What does it look like? And what position were you in as you wrote? As with the place in which this imagined activity took place, the writing tool and surface may be actual or fictive or contain elements of both, and can evoke a variety of other memories. Like the place, the composite image of writing tool, style, and surface may change, but it does retain its own distinct impression.

The complexity of your commemorative exercise becomes both more apparent and more obscure. Taking the hint from Freud, you may wonder why the image appeared in a particular way and not another, and what meanings it might conceal. But the intricacy of the image precedes any in-depth psychological or other analysis, and brings with it its own style and "language" of manifest and hidden significances. What seems a merely technical procedure quickly opens into a presence with its own life, far-reaching in its suggestiveness. Within the place and image that present themselves to your field of awareness, there are hints and glimpses of many other places and images—places and images that open to others.

Whether spontaneously experienced or deliberately practiced, psychological commemoration provides *houses* for images, places in which they can dwell. Gaston Bachelard has probed some of the many interrelations between house, memory, forgetting, and psyche. "Taking the house as a *tool for analysis* of the human soul," he observes that "Not only our memories, but the things we have forgotten are 'housed.' Our soul is an abode. And by remembering 'houses' and 'rooms,' we learn to 'abide' within ourselves."[8] Moreover, the house gives precise shape and location to memory: "thanks to the house, a great many of our memories are housed, and if the house is a bit elaborate, if it has a cellar and a garret, nooks and corridors, our memories have refuges that are all the more clearly delineated. A psychoanalyst should, therefore, turn his attention to this simple localization of our memories." The House of Memory provides a subtler ecological image for the interrelationships of memory and forgetting than our usual way of splitting them into opposite poles.

This house is not confined to that of literal reality; "the real houses of memory, the houses to which we return in dreams, the houses that are rich in unalterable oneirism, do not readily lend themselves to description[;] . . . the oneiric house," says Bachelard, "must retain its shadows." And these "houses that were lost forever continue to live on in us . . . they insist in us in order to live again, as though they expected us to give them a supplement of living. . . . How suddenly our memories assume a living possibility of being!"

The "house" in which psychological commemoration takes place is also not confined to familiar or domestic places (though it never excludes those places either); it has larger and stranger dimensions. Remember the invocative and ritual images of Animal and Plant People in Anasazi and Kwakiutl constructions. It happens that ecology itself bespeaks a place of housing, deriving as it does from the Greek *oikos,* "house." And memory houses imaginations that range far from our usual territories: dreamtime imaginations. Its shadows and intricacies, like those of any ecosystem, like those of a dream, can never be fully known. It is like the "dream's navel" of which Freud speaks in connection with his famous "Irma" dream of late July, 1895—"the first dream which I submitted for a detailed interpretation," the initiatory dream of psychoanalysis. The navel is where wonder emerges—"the spot where [the dream] reaches down into the unknown."[9]

In an imaginatively open house, the Unknown also reaches in. For instance, Loren Eiseley remembers that "As a boy I once rolled dice in an empty house, playing against myself. I suppose I was afraid. It was twilight, and I forget who won. I was too young to have known that the old abandoned house in which I played was the universe."[10] Bachelard too recognizes that the house "is our first universe, a real cosmos in every sense of the word,"[11] as does Marsilio Ficino, a Renaissance practitioner of the art of memory, in suggesting that: "Deep inside your house you might set up a little room, one with an arch, and mark it all up with . . . figures and colors" that mark it as "an image of the universe itself[.]" [12]The movement in the tradition of the art of memory is from literally housing images in buildings (in the classical Latin period) toward a recognition (among Renaissance neo-Platonists and alchemists) that images are housed metaphorically in physiognomic features of the world—that the world is the House of Memory.

This movement returns us to an ecological awareness—a living sense that within the microcosm of each particular image is a great world, a macrocosm, and that the world's strangeness is alive and at work within our most intimately familiar and domestic lives.

Psychological commemoration becomes, through its close concentration upon the impressions of images, a way of making particular, local places houses for the foreign, the planetary, the cosmic—a way of undoing polar oppositions between the domestic and the far-away while yet remembering distinctions among them. For no matter how far we travel, or how narrow the limits we set upon our imaginations, we remain in the House of Memory, housed deep inside the world.

4

The Art of Memory: "Rules for Mourning"

The "rules" for practicing the art of memory can provide a structural basis for psychological commemoration. Yet, however literally we follow these, they remain metaphors as well—metaphors that, according to what figures as the "origin myth" of the art, function specifically to enable mourning.

Cicero tells us the story of how the art of memory began.[1] It is set in classical Greece, in the sixth-century B.C.E, a time when, as now, people sought ways of leaving lasting impressions of themselves. With that in mind, a certain nobleman named Scopas decides to have a banquet, and hires a poet, Simonides, to sing a panegyric in his honor. At the occasion, with all the guests gathered around the table, Simonides does what he is hired to do, but also what he is hired, in effect, not to do—praise others as well. Specifically, Castor and Pollux, the twin brothers and sons of Zeus. This makes Scopas so angry that he tells Simonides he will pay him only half the fee agreed upon, adding sarcastically that the poet might obtain the rest from Castor and Pollux. At this point a mysterious messenger appears, and tells Simonides that two young men outside the banquet hall wish to see him. He goes outside but sees no one.

At that moment the roof of the banquet hall collapses, killing everyone except Simonides. The bodies, in fact, are so mutilated that relatives cannot identify them. It is Simonides's memory that allows for proper funeral rites, for he had kept in memory the order in which the ill-fated guests sat, enabling him to identify the victims in their places. Thus Simonides discovers the basic rules of art of memory: one holds in memory a particular order of places, with a mnemonic image housed in each.

Not exactly images chosen at random. The art of memory is founded on a story about an absurd, seemingly chance catastrophe involving grotesque death. Disfigured images will be seen as particularly valuable for the memory, which, in turn, brings order into a horrifying situation of death and loss. While the value of the visual imagination is often stressed in later *ars memorativa* treatises, there is that which does not meet the eye here. For in the background are the twin sons of Zeus, who remain invisible to Simonides. This means that the poet is saved by the appearance of the Unseen. The unseen reality has to do with brothers, one of whom is mortal (Castor) while the other (Pollux) is immortal—though the immortal twin shares in the death of the other and vice versa. For the two brothers spend one day in the tomb, the house of Hades; and the next in heaven. Alternating between life and death, they are, according to an ancient logic of myth, moon-brothers. The art of memory at times takes us into an in-between realm, where one experiences the moon-like—part immortal and part mortal—quality of the psyche. It is in that realm, "seeing" death in its visible and occult ramifications, that the art of memory finds its place.

This story embodies the mythic pattern that practitioners of the art of memory must in some way follow. Present here are foundational relations between memory, death, and human continuity. From death arises the necessity of remembering: the dead must be "placed" in memory if what is lasting is to be kept alive, and the dead themselves suitably commemorated, mourned. Simonides's discovery of the principles of the art of memory presupposes his granting a place in the remembering of his song to the twins;

through his gift of mythic remembrance a "brotherly" relation of the mortal and the immortal becomes efficacious, saving the poet as the others sit at table unaware of the peril overshadowing them. And we are given the gift of the art of memory by Simonides's having gone back after the disaster and seen death, which seeing granted a place for the profound sorrow of survivors.

In order for this deeper and mournful remembrance to take place, Simonides must first offend a narrower form of memory—an intensified remembering of the self, which cancels awareness both of the importance of others and, as the story implies, one's own vulnerability and peril. Scopas's consequent anger echoes through later struggles over memory and commemoration, through the corridors of the Smithsonian Institution and the Hiroshima Peace Museum. In the art of memory's foundational story, an exclusive focus on *self*-commemoration gives way to a primary (though not exclusive) focus on the commemoration of the dead, of souls. The latter focus is the distinguishing feature of psychological commemoration.

There is something austere in the way the unknown author of the earliest-known detailed treatise on the "rules" for memory "places" (*loci*) and "images" (*imagines*) addresses his subject.[2] Place yourself in the shoes of the classical orator seeking to enter the Treasure House of Memory. First you search for memory loci, seeking out buildings with easily remembered places, for instance "a house, an intercolumnar space, a corner, an arch, or the like." Carefully, slowly, you meditate on the precise details of each place until you have memorized it. You proceed from place to place in an order appropriate to the images that will inhabit each. You move in solitude, since the distractions of crowds tend to weaken the impression of the (place-) images. (Remember the boy Brent Staples, forming impressions of his surroundings, and then being interrupted: "Hey, you, wake up!") Having memorized the loci, you can move through them starting from any place and find the images, with their embodied information, in the right order. For the loci, our author tells us, are like wax tablets and the images like the letters impressed upon these; the images can be removed or effaced so that the "tablets" of loci can be "written" upon again.

Whether the places are actual or fictive or a combination of both, they should be well-lit (but not too bright), so the images will stand out sharply. They should be spaced at moderate intervals, "approximately thirty feet; for, like the external eye, so the inner eye of thought is less powerful when you have moved the object of sight too near or too far away." They should likewise bear distinguishing features in order to avoid confusion, and for the same reason you might mark every fifth and tenth place with a special feature, for instance a golden hand and an image of an acquaintance named "Decimus."

Let's stop here for a moment, and get acquainted with Decimus. For, both as a character and as a placename, *Decimus* remembers an interesting history. Is there in this name an echo of the art of memory's origin myth, which is located in a scene of decimation? It surely echoes the classical Roman practice of punishing every tenth individual in a regiment charged with mutiny, treason, or other offense. To decimate also meant to *tax*; it was in later and poetic usage that it came to mean "to almost completely exterminate." So Decimus could then be, or evoke, a wounded, disfigured, dead or dying character—in accordance with the "rules" for images. The art of memory is a place for images of the punished, taxed, and decimated. And, notably, those who are treasonous to imperial aims.

As a placename, Decimus embodies the link between a particular place and its inhabiting image or character(s), and highlights the crucial role of place experiences in the art of memory. Its practices, in all their variety, involve direct experiences of psychic interiority, of the *soul as place*—or many places—"within" which one moves as one remembers. The remembered places of the soul constitute a kind of pre-Freudian psychic topography, but without an overarching topographical model. Instead we find a numberless variety of featured places, and they beckon to us. We'll visit Decimus again.

Anticipating—and perhaps inspiring—Dante, our unknown author next advises us that the mnemonic figures should take on bizarre, emotionally striking shapes. For "nature herself teaches us what we should do." Marvelous or horrible events and weird, distorted or fabulous images are most effective in stirring the soul, its emotions and memories, while "we generally fail to remember" the ordinary, or the emotionally insignificant.

> We ought, then, to set up images of a kind that can adhere longest in the memory. And we shall do so if we establish likenesses that are as striking as possible; if we set up images that are not many or vague, but doing something; if we assign to them exceptional beauty or singular ugliness; if we dress some of them with crowns or purple cloaks, for example, so that the likeness may be more distinct to us; or if we somehow disfigure them, as by introducing one stained with blood or soiled with mud or smeared with red paint, so that its form is more striking, or by assigning certain comic effects to our images, for that, too, will ensure our remembering them more readily.[3]

These are *active* images, agents of imagination's impressive activities—"dramatically engaged," as Frances Yates says, alluding to their dramaturgical power—"doing something."[4] What teaches us here is the *psychological* nature of memory and its primary processes: distortions, displacements, overdeterminations. James Hillman draws a parallel between the practice of the art of memory and individuals' images from dream, fantasy, and psychic travail, with their "exact pathological details."[5]

The strange predicaments of memory images flower fully in the contortions described in Dante's *Inferno*. Try placing yourself in the shoes of fortune tellers and diviners in the eighth circle of Hell:

> And when I looked down from their faces, I saw
> that each of them was hideously distorted
> between the top of the chest and the lines of the jaw;

for the face was reversed on the neck, and they came on
backwards, staring backwards at their loins,
for to look before them was forbidden. Someone,

sometime, in the grip of a palsy may have been
distorted so, but never to my knowledge
nor do I believe the like was ever seen. (XX. 10-8)

As with all the figures of the *Inferno*, these distortions stand in an
exact symbolic relationship to the sins committed in life. "Thus,"
as John Ciardi comments, "those who sought to penetrate the
future cannot even see in front of themselves; they attempted to
move themselves forward in time, so must they go backwards
through all eternity; and as the arts of sorcery are a distortion of
God's law, so are their bodies distorted in Hell."[6]

It is a strange devotion we remember here. That Dante's
remembering of these images is deeply devotional is evident not
only through the context of his medieval theology and cosmology;
it is also revealed by his awe in the face of their strangeness: "nor
do I believe the like was ever seen." *To be devoted to the remembering of images in deepest pain*: this form of devotion may appear not
just strange but grotesque; "the mediaeval love of the grotesque" is
rarely remembered.[7] But it has its place in memory: a place shared
with deep ethical and moral concern. For it has always been the
case that something in "the soul is moved most profoundly by
images that are disfigured, unnatural, and in pain."[8] Moved, that is,
by what calls our attention to loss, by the desire of mourning.

Though the images to which previous practitioners of the art of
memory draw our attention may be strange, contorted, or grotesque, that does not mean beauty is absent. The art of memory
requires an Aphrodisiac sensibility, a loving engagement with the
sensual surfaces of images, or an awareness of the Aphrodisiac
qualities inherent in imagination. It involves a discerning sense of
"taste" and "feel" for places and images and a love of their meta-

phoric shapes as well as a careful eye as to their features and placing.

Part of the beauty of this art of imagination is precisely its inclusion of "singular ugliness," "blood," "mud" (to use the images of the old memory treatise), and the suffering. Beauty itself need not be literalized—as Aphrodite, Goddess of Beauty, is herself prone to do. The vanity of Beauty—its unblemished purity—can cause or contribute to wars. The former, it is said, was the case in the Trojan War, and the latter figured in the lead-up to Hitler's war. Remember the grace and beauty of the photographs and films of Leni Reifenstahl, and of other figures who come to embody the beautified identity of a given group.

Aphrodite herself cannot exclude what contradicts ideal beauty; she also gives birth to the monstrous child, Priapus, who sports a huge, misshapen penis, protruding belly and tongue.[9] Though Aphrodite rejects him, she is still his mother: the love of the beautiful is inescapably related to the "love of the grotesque," which deepens Aphrodisiac consciousness not by moving *beneath* image-surfaces (that is, eschewing their precise forms in favor of more abstract, seemingly "deeper" interpretive categories), but rather erotically toward those surfaces, shapes and faces scorned by a too literal or ideal notion of beauty. There are ugly, grotesque, painful and freakish images that bring depth to beauty and render aesthetic sensitivity psychological. This is well-illustrated by the beauty of Dante's *Inferno*.

Such images often harbor remembrances of what we more usually think of as beautiful, or echoes of the lost. Grotesque images may be images in mourning—perhaps that's part of their striking power. Again, the images are by no means always *literally* grotesque or odd or in pain—they may be overtly beautiful or merely ordinary, but have ugly or disturbing implications.

Philosopher Alphonso Lingis, meditating on one's encounters with suffering others, eloquently expresses the careful and caring attentiveness inherent in an Aphrodisiac openness to others' worlds:

The surfaces of the other, as surfaces of susceptibility and suffering, are felt in the caressing movement that troubles my exploring, manipulating, and expressive hand. For the hand that caresses is not investigating, does not gather information, is not a sense organ. It extends over a surface where the informative forms soften and sink away as it advances, where agitations of alien pleasure and pain surface to meet it and move it. The hand that caresses does not apprehend or manipulate; it is not an instrument. It extends over a surface which blocks the way to the substance while giving way everywhere; it extends over limbs which have abandoned their utility and their intentions. The hand that caresses does not communicate a message. It advances repetitively, aimlessly, and indefatigably, not knowing what it wants to say, where it is going, or why it has come here. In its aimlessness it is passive, in its agitation it no longer moves itself; it is moved by the passivity, the suffering, the torments of pleasure and pain, of the other.[10]

Having reviewed the "rules" for the art of memory and their roots in mythic narrative, let us now observe them in practical illustrations of psychological commemoration, feeling our way with "the hand that caresses." The first of the two following passages is from a twentieth-century practitioner of the art of memory. I doubt whether he had the literal "rules" for its practice in mind, but his—and, therefore, his reader's—imaginations adhere to them rather closely, attending to the exact details of the places his imagination's eye revisits and to the characters that people each place. The second, italicized passage recounts one episode of my personal work with psychological commemoration. Further recountings of my explorations, also set off in italics, will follow later.

Our first example takes place "At exactly fifteen minutes past eight in the morning, on August 6, 1945, Japanese time":

at the moment when the atomic bomb flashed above
Hiroshima, Miss Toshiko Sasaki, a clerk in the personal
department of the East Asia Tin Works, had just sad down
at her place in the plant office and was turning her head to
speak to the girl at the next desk. At that same moment,
Dr. Masakazu Fujii was settling down cross-legged to read
the Osaka *Asahi* on the porch of his private hospital,
overhanging one of the seven deltaic rivers which divide
Hiroshima; Mrs. Hatsuyo Nakamura, a tailor's widow,
stood by the window of her kitchen, watching a neighbor
tearing down his house because it lay in the path of an air-
raid-defense fire lane; Father Wilhelm Kleinsorge, a German
priest of the Society of Jesus, reclined in his underwear on
a cot on the top floor of his order's three-story mission
house, reading a Jesuit magazine, *Stimmen der Zeit;* Dr.
Terufumi Sasaki, a young member of the surgical staff of
the city's large, modern Red Cross Hospital, walked along
one of the hospital corridors with a blood specimen for a
Wasserman test in his hand; and the Reverend Mr. Kiyoshi
Tanimoto, pastor of the Hiroshima Methodist Church,
paused at the door of a rich man's house in Koi, the city's
western suburb, and prepared to unload a handcart full of
things he had evacuated from town in fear of the massive
B-29 raid which everyone expected Hiroshima to suffer.[11]

This passage is recognizable both as the beginning of John
Hersey's *Hiroshima,* and as an illustration of the spontaneous
organization of memory in patterns of places and images. It also
marked, when it appeared in *The New Yorker* in 1946, one of
history's largest-scale commemorative imaginations of the humanity
of people from a far shore, on "the other side." It is for this reason
that Hersey's account, strengthened by its deft combination of
precise memorial detail with grace and restraint, is itself worthy of
commemoration; in effect, *Hiroshima* involves the reader in an
extended exercise of psychological commemoration, of intensified

and hospitable remembering of strangers. The spirits of Hiroshima will speak to us if we allow them into our own homes of imagination and memory—if we befriend them.

I feel a nervous tingling in my hands, and it makes me want to dance and jump. I imagine myself doing so. Or I actually do so, now imagining myself and observing any changes that take place as I dance and jump. In this movement of bodily imagination, I notice the presence of another image. It is a picture in a volume of watercolors called Unforgettable Fire, *drawn by one of those who, in the terms of Hersey's Hiroshima, was a member of the group referred to by others as the "bomb people." It is of a victim whose hands were badly burnt, so that the skin hangs in strips from the fingertips. He stands, outstretched, in the street; to his right are piles of flaming rubble. I now feel this image and its exquisite pain with and in my fingers and yet, as I feel it, it becomes distinguished from "my" self, inhabiting a place that is both distinct from and related to my own.*

How can the image be real? For no actual person in such a position would want to dance and jump. Accounts of the atomic bombing, in fact, depict bomb victims with burnt skin hanging from their fingertips, walking slowly, trying to avoid any friction that would add to the pain. In fantasy, though, the urge to dance, which this image presents to me, seems a way of accentuating both the pain and its awareness; this I get in touch with through the fingertips. The fantasy person seems to want this, to want to articulate a dance of pain, a movement of suffering in ritual, which opens into the felt woundedness of image and of actual history. One of the Bomb People lives again, reminding me of what actual people suffered in the Hiroshima and Nagasaki bombings—and reminding me as well that somewhere the same suffering must still be present, that it has a future, remains to be mourned.

Gaston Bachelard observes that "Memories are motionlessness, and the more securely they are fixed in space, the sounder they are."[12] Memories remain in place if they are to remain as memories. According to the "rules" of the art of memory, the images, however active, are fixed in their places. Memory immobilizes the imagination—kills it. The souls with their heads facing backwards in the eighth circle of the Inferno are still there today, in the same place. We are returned to the foundation of the art, the scene of the disastrous banquet: The soul is moved to remember by death. Death moves us by not moving; rendered motionless, imagination is moved, remembered.

This is meant literally and metaphorically. For though we are instructed to literally "fix" images in their places, we have to move around in order to do so. The images also move around with us—because they are fixed in their places. James Hillman notes that in the art of memory there is a kind of "inactive imagination" in which events are carried, held and digested "inside" so that "space is created to contain them."[13] Precisely because they are fixed in one place, these memorial images can walk about, can inhabit many places simultaneously. In some of those places, they are not, *overtly*, motionless, but move about in the field of imagination, engaged in whatever they are doing.

An overtly moving image can be at the same time motionless on the occult level. This is the case with the Reverend Mr. Kyoshi Tanimoto of *Hiroshima*. Hersey describes him with characteristic precision: "He wears his black hair parted in the middle and rather long: the prominence of his mustache, mouth and chin give him a strange, old-young look, boyish and yet wise, weak and yet fiery."[14] Mr. Tanimoto sustained few physical injuries in the bombing, and was intensely active in its aftermath, ferrying people in a boat across a branch of the Ota River to a safer place in Hiroshima's Asano Park.

He is old-young, boyish-wise, weak-fiery: Hersey's description of these paradoxically present qualities evokes a liminal figure, one who moves in more than one world. Which is precisely what his rescue activity required of him. As the firestorm following the bombing spread, he

> walked to the river and began to look for a boat in which he might carry some of the most severely injured across the river from Asano Park and away from the spreading fire. Soon he found a good-sized pleasure punt drawn up on the bank, but in and around it was an awful tableau—five dead men, nearly naked, badly burned, who must have been working together to push the boat down into the river. Mr. Tanimoto lifted them away from the boat, and as he did so, he experienced such horror at disturbing the dead— preventing them, he momentarily felt, from launching their craft and going on their ghostly way—that he said out loud, "Please forgive me for taking this boat. I must use it for others, who are alive."[15]

For the remainder of "that day," as it was called, Mr. Tanimoto, using for propulsion a bamboo pole he finds, ferries boatloads of wounded people, ten to twelve at a time across the river to the park. In the evening, continuing his work, the "ferryman" (Hersey's characterization) transports a pair of wounded priests upstream to where they can get to the Jesuit Novitiate outside of Hiroshima.[16]

Mr. Tanimoto thus becomes another, archetypal Person—the Ferryman who takes and pilots the vessel of the dead who are about to go "on their ghostly way." And the living whom this Ferryman brings to the other shore are themselves Walking Ghosts in the Land on the Far Side of Forgetfulness. This Ferryman and the topography of his world are well-known in the world's myth, folklore, and accounts (such as Plato's *Republic*) of the soul's ecstatic journeys.[17] Dante and others see the classical Ferryman Charon in his "ancient ferry"[18] as he takes souls across the river Acheron on their way to their new homes, and we might remember as well the *yana* or "raft" of Buddhism, which vehicle provides for the extinguishment of desire, the journey to the Other Shore and *nirvana*.

It is a mythic ecology that structures Hersey's reconstruction of *Hiroshima*. We find there the Ferryman, the ghostly craft or vessel of death, the river, the dead and the dead-in-life, who are taken from the City of Death to the Other Shore. As this mythic ecology is remembered, so too is the historical ecology of nuclear horror. The 1946 publication of Hersey's account was for many—in a sense, for the world—a rite of passage into the era of Death-in-Life, a conjunction of timeless reality and unique historical predicament.[19] Asano Park, the safer place, may be in one sense the place of rescue, but it is also the safe place of death. Mr. Tanimoto's transports are at once strenuous efforts at ensuring survival and movements toward, and within, a topography of death. It is Ferryman's *movement* that reveals his fixed place within that topography—the Forever within the historical actuality of Hiroshima.

"Every image ferries you between a Here and a There," says the spirit of Hiroshima. It is 3a.m. and I'm unable to sleep. I go into the kitchen for some water and there, facing me from the semi-dark of my livingroom, is the man with his arms outstretched and skin hanging from them in strips. This is what he wants to say: Every image, every memory, carries you between lands of life and death. Your home is at the same time a foreign country.

Now it is August of 1992; I am in a hotel on the shores of the Baltic Sea in St. Petersburg, Russia. Hiroshima, the spirit, is with me. I remember now an American businessman and a Russian psychologist discussing the Russian predicament, each—with the best intentions—condescending to the other. The American wants to illustrate the A B C's of managing a market economy; the Russian is illustrating a lack of spiritual culture in America. Each looks down upon the other's lack of experience and is at the same time in awe of the other's wealth of experience, but they only manage to talk past each other.

Each man is being wounded by the other, but only the

spirit of Hiroshima fully feels this. For his flame-flayed fingers are minutely sensitive to everything in his environment so that no pain can escape him. He cannot escape the friction in the room; it charges through his hands matter how still he remains. He cannot but remain mindful of "the chafe and jar/of nuclear war" which so disturbed Robert Lowell; he remembers that anxieties evocative of Hiroshima form part of the backdrop of Russian-American (and other intergroup) frictions. The Russian and American can sense the pain too, though less acutely—they are hurting each other in order to ward it off. They are together in a small hotel room but on separate psychological shores.

Hiroshima wants to say that persisting difficulties in Russian-American relations, as with other forms of friction between foreign and familiar, begins anew each moment, in one's resistance to the ferrying power of the other's images. People try to cling to one shore only, because they are under the illusion of its exclusive familiarity and do not wish to remember that every place is also a foreign country. To condescend to another is to try to domesticate the other, and to try and keep oneself from being ferried to the shore of foreign wildness. To befriend another is to allow a place in oneself for their strangeness. There is still friction but you are able, and may on occasion desire, to dance together.

Marsilio Ficino once complained to a friend about the malign influence of the melancholy God Saturn in his life. His friend responded by pointing out that along with the burden of sadness, Saturn's melancholy gives one "a comprehensive memory, in which all things are present in correct time and place."[20] Earlier writers, such as the Scholastic theologian Albert the Great, would have concurred. Albert observes that there is a particular form of melancholy that inspires; it is sanguine, choleric—passionate. Those upon whom Saturn visits this form of melancholy are moved most by what Albert calls *phantasmata*—the fantasy-images required by the art of "reminiscence."[21] And the writer of the earlier memory treatise, we'll remember, advises us: "It will be more advantageous to obtain [loci] in a deserted than in a populous region, because the crowding and passing to and fro of people confuse and weaken the impress of the images, while solitude keeps their outlines sharp."[22] There is in this image a distinctly melancholy aura.

Solitude is meant literally here, but it can also be reflective of processes of separation going on in the soul—of withdrawal from former images ("the crowding . . . of people") so that others may be more intensely imagined, memorialized. This is what goes on when people mourn, as Freud explained in his paper "On Mourning and Melancholia": the psychic work of detachment from relationship to a newly dead person develops into the re-creative power of memorial images connected with the deceased, now held in places of the soul, commemorated.[23] And, in the work of mourning, places that evoke loss and the presence of the dead become more important, are repeatedly revisited in imagination. This reminds us of the art of memory's rules for place, which, in Frances Yates's words, "summon up a vision of a forgotten social habit. Who is that man moving slowly in the lonely building stopping at intervals with an intent face? He is a rhetoric student forming a set of memory loci."[24] The imaginative cultivation of memory is an occasion for slow going, frequent stopping and being in a lonely place: contemplating and imagining places. The art of memory is a work of melancholy; its rules, like Brent Staples's meditative concentration on place images against a backdrop of loss and displacement—and like psychological commemoration in general—follow psychic pathways of the mourning process.

5

A Deeper Form of Forgetting

In the work of psychological commemoration, as in that of mourning, it is not only "we" who remember; others remember through us as well. Psychological commemoration means not only that we are remembering images, but also that images are *themselves* rememberings: memory is inherent in their being. Our work means giving images a place within which they can carry on *their* work of remembering through us. Which is why, in mourning the death of a loved one, we so often imagine and remember how they might view and experience our ongoing lives and those of others. And we, as well, are images, housed in memory's multitudinous places. To realize this means to carry the movement away from exclusive self-commemoration a step farther, to cultivate, together with a more intricate and imaginative memory, that deep and necessary form of forgetting which allows for the commemoration of souls.

In contrast to the forgetfulness of group memory, this form of forgetting involves an intensified imagining of the psyche's outsiders, a form of empathetic engagement with them. A closer consideration of this intensified imagining will deepen our appreciation of role of forgetting in psychological commemoration.

In characterizing the art of memory as an "inactive imagination," James Hillman tellingly alludes to the practice, in Jungian psychoanalysis, of "active imagination." Active imagination was developed by Jung and described in his autobiographical account of his initiatory "confrontation with the unconscious," his near-breakdown that resulted from his breakup with Freud. Jung's encounter with madness involved more than his personal psychology; it took place during the time around World War I and included (in the autumn of 1913) explicit visions of "a frightful catastrophe" in Europe. His psychological explorations included frequent imaginings of "a steep descent" into a place he felt was "the land of the dead" (like Brent Staples, who on seeing the photographs of his dead brother "fell down and down for miles"); and the dead themselves he imagined "as the voices of the Unanswered, Unresolved, and Unredeemed . . ."[1] The place might also be imagined as where Hiroshima dwells—together with all the unanswered, unresolved, unredeemed questions and imaginations that arise in us with regard to our massive violence.

Psychological commemoration has much in common with active imagination, the latter being self-evidently a form of intensified imagining. Active imagination is initiated by concentrating upon a fantasy image (one that spontaneously comes to mind, not an externally-suggested one), carefully noticing how it changes and allowing it its own autonomy and intentions. Then you can "speak" with the figure in some manner and listen to what the figure may have to say to you. Both your habitual self and the imaginal other thus assume active roles. At the same time, another part of yourself can observe the imaginative interplay, recognizing it as a dialogue in which different parts of the personality can confront each other, becoming both more distinct and more integrated. It can later be written down, and can be concretely enacted through dance, visual media, music, or poetry.

Jungian analysts have characterized active imagination with the German term *auseinandersetzung*—a kind of "coming-to-terms with another."[2] The prefix *aus*—outside, or foreign, as in *auslander*, foreigner—is especially significant, drawing attention to ways in which the figures encountered in active imagination remain outside one's habitual self. This respect for the status of the outsider is equally important in psychological commemoration.

But such commemoration focuses our attention on the *unchanging* as well as changing qualities of psychological experience—the qualities of memory Bachelard calls "motionless." Its imaginations are intensified precisely because, paralleling the art of memory, they remain mindful of a distinct and paradoxical *in*activity of images. This, in turn, heightens awareness of the containing and defining powers of place—the need of imagination for multiple locations.

The activities of *Hiroshima's* Mr. Tanimoto speak to us in this regard. In one memorial place (not visually present in consciousness), his old-young figure may stand still—his face animated yet motionless—while in another place, you carry on a dialogue with him (let us say he is visually imagined here, but this is not necessary). He speaks, and then you speak in turn, later writing down the dialogue. You move in imagination between the still and moving images, which act to define and intensify each other.

The intricacy of the dialogue may grow, its multiple players become evident. For instance, the back-and-forth moving of Ferryman's vessel across the River of Death may be present in the background (perhaps as a *thought* or intimation combined with a faint feel of water and memories of the bodily rhythm and sounds of rowing, but not as a visual image) as you face Mr. Tanimoto and speak with him. And the movement of the boat of the dead behind the dramatic scene is itself a static form, an inactive image. But it quickens our awareness of life's unceasing movement toward the Land of Forever.

Whatever its form, psychological commemoration combines the "intrapsychic memorialization" identified by Edward Casey in connection with Freud's "Mourning and Melancholia" with a recognition of the mythic ecology of memory images and of their partially foreign character. It honors those images—gives their metaphoric depths and precision the gift of our attentive care. It is an act of friendship.

Moreover, the special intensity of commemorative remembering means that the images remembered (and remembering) gain new power in our psychological lives. Referring to Freud's notion of the "deferred action" (*Nachträglichkeit*) of certain memories in the context of new circumstances, Casey points toward instances of remembering in which "the later vision is inherently stronger—more lasting, more forceful—than the first vision."[3] During the course of psychological commemoration, images associated with Hiroshima, or any place, can become more potent than when they were first impressed on our imaginations; their effects will thus become "more lasting, more forceful."

> *I come to feel the spirit of Hiroshima as my friend. I can't put my finger on it, but somehow his presence reassures. For, despite his terrible burns, he abides, in many places. He is there standing on the street in the watercolor painting, the blackened rubble to his right; he is there as well in the semi-dark, dead-of-night time in my own living place. And he accompanies me to different places, as when we revisited the Russian-American conversation I witnessed in 1992 in St. Petersburg. I learn something from his presence; he embodies the metaphoric presence of Hiroshima in more recent events—what Hiroshima has to say to us now.*

How do these impressions gain force? There is, first, the attentive care and sense of reciprocal relationship one accords the places and images. This attention catalyzes their activity, as in the overt process of active imagination. But here is also where *forgetfulness* gets involved—a forgetting which enables the ongoing deepening of the work of memory. Initially, this form of forgetting is what enables us to be more open to unconventional, strange, or difficult images; it helps us let go of conventional assumptions regarding what images are, and are not, valuable. In the work of psychological commemoration, we temporarily forget the normalized world; forgetfulness realizes its place as genuine liminal terrain, between lands of life and death. We locate ourselves in No One's Land.

Nonetheless, the images housed through psychological commemoration of Hiroshima are not often images we will want to, or even be capable of, carrying consciously with us through the course of our daily lives (though, like literature's memorable characters, they may at times emerge unexpectedly into awareness, and we can visit their places). Immersion in profound sorrow cannot be permanently conscious in its full intensity. As in the work of mourning, some kind of separation, some degree of forgetfulness, must take place over time. But the forgetfulness of genuine mourning is precisely its *work*—the construction of suitable shelters for sorrow, for memories. Recall Bachelard's statement that "Not only our memories, but the things we have forgotten are 'housed.'" After we have housed in memory images that sadden us, these figures continue to live in their houses even though our attention is far more frequently focused on other affairs. Having been housed, they abide with us even when we do not notice. They are now in place, cared for and attended; though we may return to them, and they to us, their remaining housed in memory does not require our constant, or even frequent, recollective attention.

The distinction, in Edward Casey's terms, between "recollective [and conscious] remembering" and an "Ongoing, steady remembering" which for the most part proceeds outside of conscious awareness, is basic to an understanding of psychological commemoration.[4] There is an essential part of the work of memory that, far from requiring a continual and all-inclusive (ego-) consciousness, requires a degree of hiddenness; it goes on behind the "scenes" of recollective (and, as usually imagined, visual) remembering. A "forgetting" of recollective memory of the place of Hiroshima is necessary not only, and not primarily, so that we can get on with the activities of daily living. Instead, the images need to be allowed their own space so that they may impress themselves in their own ways, effectively setting up their own houses in memory. They are then present with us, largely hidden, invisible, yet potent and lasting, powers dwelling within our lives.

How do these places and images become such relatively permanent, though usually invisible, presences within our world(s)? Through the further work of mourning, as Casey observes. This work involves psychological processes of *incorporation* of others into one's psychic sphere, hence of the *identification* of aspects of oneself with these others, and finally of their establishment as fully *internalized* presences "hidden" within our personalities. Psychoanalyst Edward Emery speaks in this connection of the *implacement* of others' presences in one's psychic space—a process that seems reflected in Casey's observation that "Each of these presences brings about a new place in the psyche—a new memorial location that, far from freezing the past into fixity, opens ever more expansively into the future."[5] (There is a place for frozen fixity in psychological commemoration, but because the psyche's frozen places are dramatically engaged, we are freed from exclusively literalized attachments—like those of right-wing American and Japanese veterans and politicians—to idealized, "fixed" images of the past that freeze out history's dramatic complexity.) It is in this opening that the ecology of mourning is most fully realized.

The groundwork for this psychic expansiveness is laid in our initial recognition of multiple levels of metaphor within the places and images we set out to commemorate. It is through the cultivation of this psychic and imaginative expansiveness that I believe the psychological commemoration of Hiroshima can indirectly help in the formulation of nonviolent cultural organization(s), laying their foundations by undermining the spiritual and ethical confinement of group self-commemoration and replacing it with a profounder form of forgetting. A form of letting-go, of opening our memories to the world's deeper and broader expanses. A way of commemorating the world itself.

6

Hiroshima: Place and Time

Think about Hiroshima My Love—the scene from the movie in which the Japanese man and the French woman are in bed and Hiroshima is with them. The man says: "You have seen nothing in Hiroshima. Nothing." The woman says: "I have seen everything. Everything."[1] No, nothing, says the man, who lost his family to the bomb. His insistence can be taken to mean, as one psychoanalyst suggests, that "*We* have seen nothing in Hiroshima"—an expression of shared denial of the true impact and extent of the loss and its implications. But it is also an expression of psychological truth. "Everything" and "Nothing" are only seeming opposites. To be intimate with Hiroshima is to see Nothing, and Everything. *Hiroshima Mon Amour*: the place of desperate lovemaking and anguished conflict between Everything and Nothing—where the parties join and struggle and fall apart together.

We can learn more about the nature of the place of Hiroshima by revisiting another scene—that of the disaster which gives rise to the art of memory. The collapse of the roof of Scopas's banquet hall can serve not only as a concise definition of what psychological commemoration involves, but also as a parable of the nuclear predicament that began with the bombings of Hiroshima and Nagasaki. Like the banquet guests, the people of Hiroshima went about their business on the morning of the bomb, not knowing the peril hanging over their heads. The bomb fell; the roof fell in, leaving a site of horrible, grotesque death. A world is destroyed; the banquet is Death's own. To this site we must return, and, through the placings of memory, seek restoration of order, meaning and human continuity, giving the dead their place through mourning. But this requires a prior acknowledgment of the hidden or unseen relation of mortality and immortality in the soul, a way of dwelling like Castor and Pollux in both heaven and Hades. Simultaneously, there is a movement away from exclusive self-commemoration—from the position in which we remain, for practical purposes, unaware of, or deadened to, perils right now hanging over us. This movement is what keeps the possibilities of memory and mourning alive.

Simonides's memory of the places in which the victims sat requires something more—a memory of the place itself, a memory he must salvage from the site of decimation. This suggests another way in which the art of memory's generative disaster speaks to the nuclear age—we too must remember qualities and structures of particular places, retrieving the ability to do so from a place and time of destruction. But this leads to some questions: Just what kind of place is Hiroshima in our imaginations? Is it a place at all? Can we meaningfully speak of a site of decimation as a place, when place itself depends on boundaries and structures—literal and metaphoric—that distinguish it from other places?

Is Hiroshima a place at all? Yes: Hiroshima has (is) a place in our imaginations, one with a quite specific, even unprecedented, nature. And no: Hiroshima embodies the presence of placelessness—in contemporary technological culture specifically, and human existence generally. Or, more paradoxically, Hiroshima is the place and time in which, historically speaking, placelessness comes into existence. It is where Everything mingles with Nothing. We will better appreciate Hiroshima's memorial *temporality*, including its "timeless" qualities, if we probe the strange and conflicted intimacy of the *place* "Hiroshima," the place where

Nothing and Everything are lovers. Lovers and broken souls. In the service of understanding that love, its necessity and its broken nature, let us briefly explore the more general psychological nature of place.

Place has its own "intrinsic memorability," notes Edward Casey (the pre-eminent philosopher of place), and this memorability is what gives particular places their power. Consider sacred places, where the divine is remembered, experienced and placed in imagination. It is through memory that Native Australians, for instance, recognize in the distinct features of their lands the ecology of the sacred, physiognomies of dreamtime beings. The relation of place, memory and the power of the sacred is also shown in the story of Jacob's dream where he sees a ladder connecting heaven and earth upon which angels are ascending and descending, and in which he is spoken to by God. Upon awakening, Jacob exclaims, "How awesome is this place! This is none other than the house of God, and this is the gate of heaven" (Gen. 28:17). Jacob then sets up the stone he had used for a headrest as a marker, a monument witnessing to and commemorating the divine power there housed. We remember that place still.

Also displayed by such sacred places is what Casey describes as the "verticality" inherent in the structure of place.[2] This is evident in Jacob's dream, with its ladder and its themes of ascent and descent, and in Dante's use of the art of memory as the vehicle for his descent into hell. It also undergirds Native Australian cosmologies—at the close of the dreamtime the primordial beings went underground. Again, in ancient Shinto ritual, the *kami* or sacred presence was invited "to come down and take up its residence temporarily in the sacred place. . . . Around the sacred spot were placed stones."[3] The *kami* originally descended to a sacred tree, the place of which was later taken by the Shinto shrine. Authors on Shintoism emphasize the ecological dimension—the sense of the *powers* of mountains, rivers, rocks, trees—especially, perhaps, the forest or "place where trees grow thick" (*himorogi*), where vertical power is at its most densely prolific.[4]

Cities are also displays of the memorable power of place. Casey ponders the attractiveness of San Francisco: "it is just the sort of place you can leave your heart in. And 'heart' is . . . the ultimate place of human attachments . . ."[5] Place is located at the heart of memory, which is why the design of memorable cities can be considered a concrete form of the art of memory. Cities embody as well the vertical imagination; they contain memory-traces of the first places of connection between the human and the divine: trees, mountains, temples and shrines, which are places of contact between earth and sky; and underground places, which connect surface and depth. In addition, cities extend *horizontally* and create boundaries—both between city and outside realm, and between distinct precincts within the city itself. We have noted the importance of boundary-making in psychological commemoration. To the extent that they are well and memorably designed, cities have their own defined ecologies which nonetheless echo the places of the countryside. They are powerful places especially because they are both *meeting-places* of differing habitats and cultural worlds, and multifaceted *openings* to higher and lower realms.

Returning to the context of Hiroshima, we find that the power of place led American planners during World War II to omit Kyoto—considered uniquely rich in religious, historical and cultural memories—from their list of atomic-bomb targets. This was done out of a combination of respect for the place (especially on the part of Secretary of War Henry Stimson) and concern for the reaction of the Japanese were it destroyed; in both considerations, the power of place is fundamental.[6] We resist remembering Hiroshima and Nagasaki not only because of our tendencies to deny and avoid death and nuclear horror; this resistance may not be *ours* alone, but also the resistance of *place itself* to the destruction of its memories, of its distinct boundaries and its openings to the vertical.

Alexander Deighton, a psychiatrist who led the research team of the U. S. Strategic Bombing Survey in its December, 1945 trip to Hiroshima to study the psychological condition of atomic-bomb survivors, bespeaks in the following passages the psychological condition of Hiroshima itself, its then placeless memories. Jolted into reverie by an emotionally striking image, Deighton notes that

> Hiroshima had been a city, at first unknown to Europe and America, then a friendly source of emigrants to the United States, and finally an enemy port. It lay on a delta between the mouths of the Ota and was traversed by canals and an ancient highway that connected Kyoto in the east with Shimonoseki in the west. Close around the city stood mountains covered with red pine, while before it stretched the bay, indented with headlands and spread with islands, in places narrow and deep like a fjord. . . .[7]

He moves from Hiroshima's natural surroundings to more specific memories—memories which are not his own, but very much alive in him. For in this city "the influence of the United States was marked. On main streets there were movies and restaurants with façades that would have fitted into shopping districts of Bakersfield or San Diego." The city "was also ancient," with its "feudal castle . . . three large temples and many smaller ones and the tombs of the Asano family . . . [and] also Christian churches whose bells mingled with the temple gongs and the honking of auto horns and the rattling of trolleys."

And yet, though all this history had been collapsed into the post-bomb terrain that constituted Deighton's only actual—as distinct from vicarious—remembrances of Hiroshima, he finds himself haunted, in another reverie, by other, disturbingly immediate memory images: "The streets of Hiroshima ran through the rubble like perspective lines in a surrealist desert. From them came images of similar streets with names like 'Broadway,' 'Constitution Avenue,' 'Michigan' and 'Kearney,' and the Hiroshima scene enacted again and again between the coasts of the United States, on a larger scale, but with no detail of suffering omitted."[8] These images of streets are avenues used by place to protest its needless decimation, and that of the future.

The "perspective lines" suggest something more particular about the destruction of place. Casey draws a sharp distinction, relevant to Hiroshima, between place and site.[9] Site lacks the particularities, the specific characteristics of place that disclose the latter's power, its place in dream and memory, soul and heart. "Think of the difference," he suggests, "between being in a cityscape or landscape and becoming sensuously attuned to it, versus gazing at a map of the same placescape." Site, by contrast, is a "modification" of place, in the sense of being "non-unique and replaceable." It is without differentiation, lacking soul, power and memorability.

Nuclear weapons are an extreme expression of psychological insensitivity to the special qualities of places. Think of the computer maps guiding strategic planning. Robert Sardello, speaking of the neglected importance of remembering a city's past history, criticizes ill-considered projects of "urban renewal," quoting the architect Arthur Erikson in this context: "There is no greater machine of aggression against the city and against one's fellow man than the bulldozer."[10] "With the exception," of course, "of the nuclear warhead."

Remember again what Hiroshima looked like after the nuclear fires died down, leaving only a horizontal grid, a flattened-out line of perspective. Casey observes that: "Sites modify places by leveling them down, razing them, making them indifferently planar, so that horizontality comes to count for more than verticality."[11] Father Wilhelm Kleinsorge (the German Jesuit survivor of Hersey's *Hiroshima*) returns twelve days after the bombing to near the explosion's hypocenter where he finds "the few standing, gutted buildings only accentuating the horizontality of everything else . . ."[12] Listen to Yoto Ota, a novelist and survivor, tell of her wandering through the destroyed city:

> I reached a bridge and saw that the Hiroshima Castle had been completely leveled to the ground, and my heart shook like a great wave. . . . This destruction of the castle gave me a thought. Even if a new city should be built on this land,

the castle would never be built and added to that city. The city of Hiroshima, entirely on flat land, was made three-dimensional by the existence of the white castle, and because of this it could retain a classical flavor. Hiroshima had a history of its own. And when I thought about these things, the grief of stepping over the corpses of history pressed upon my heart.[13]

Such landmarks as the castle, revealing the historical heart of Hiroshima, are unique and irreplaceable; their leveling stirred Miss Ota's heart and memories at a time when she had become to an extent "used" to destruction and human corpses.

The leveling of Hiroshima is remembered—as Deighton's survey shows—in images of anticipated nuclear devastation. That leveling, in addition to severing vertical connections, destroyed what is basic in place's horizontal imagination: distinct boundaries, enclosures, habitations. How right we are when we say that nuclear destruction knows no boundaries. Nor, significantly, does nuclear radiation: Chernobyl and other peacetime nuclear poisonings are both remembered and prefigured in Hiroshima. Echoes of Hiroshima reverberate through subsequent exposures of human communities and ecosystems to an expanding range of toxins and environmental injuries, including, finally, the larger place violations effected by climatic upheaval and other planetwide ecological perils.[14] In this way, Hersey's description of what happens in radiation poisoning figures as an initial exposure on the part of the global body politic to *violations of place that reach us on cellular levels:* "The rays simply destroyed body cells—caused their nuclei to degenerate and broke their walls."[15]

In this light "the place of Hiroshima" seems a self-contradictory phrase. That is so, yet Hiroshima *is*, and *lays claim to*, a quite definite place in our individual and collective imaginations. More, it is a place with remarkable staying power—an archetypal image of the nuclear age. The place of Hiroshima endures through the vicissitudes of public concern about nuclear weapons; so deep is its impression on memory that we can be certain it will remain there even if nuclear weapons are eventually abolished. For *Hiroshima is the place of no place*, revealing a deep lacuna, a *placelessness*, at the heart of postindustrial culture. To this place we must nonetheless repair; within the place of memory we may allow the imagination of place itself to once more stake its claims.

Though it ended long ago, the paradoxical affair of *Hiroshima Mon Amour* yet continues—and still contains the passion that makes Hiroshima's power as place so distinctly present.

Conversely, our persisting preparedness for nuclear decimation is an ultimate expression of insult and indifference to place and its importance to the memorial heart: a form of total forgetfulness, one that annihilates all memory, all place, all time. Just here we grasp part of the reason why nuclear destruction is often called a horror "beyond imagination": it leaves no featured place to remember. And this remembering of placelessness haunts contemporary landscapes, becomes part of the ecology of our time—the postmodern time surveyed by the streets of Hiroshima in 1945.

Rooted in the time of Hiroshima, postmodern time partakes of the qualities of that place. Linking time and place yields an image of time quite different from our usual construing of temporality as abstract and linear.[16] Time gets placed; place gets "timed"—and the combinations are kaleidoscopic, yielding a prolific variety of qualities of time and place. The *place* of Hiroshima, then, is also an image of *time;* on closer consideration, however, it resolves into many different temporal locations, including the timelessness to which the frozen-handed timepieces of Hiroshima point.

It happens that the emotionally striking image that jolted Alexander Deighton into reverie was one of those timepieces—a white-faced clock on the wall, "its hands pointing to 8:10, the time it had stopped on August 6."[17] At a moment when he felt his own emotions flattening out, the image of the clock returned to view, "like a huge fish swimming out of vague green into sharp focus," prodding him to remember "the years when that clock had been going . . ." The clock was in fact slow—the "official" time of the bomb's explosion is, as the ever-present watch says, 8:15 AM. But, like the watch, it quickens its viewer's emotions. It forces one to remember that the bombing of Hiroshima took place in historical time, that the memories of its victims are forever with us. It is, in the fullest sense of the *ars memorativa* tradition, a memory image, drawing on and emerging from oceanic depths.

Hiroshima as *time* is no single entity. The stopped hands of Hiroshima time move us to remember the future as well as present and past. As surely as they point toward seas of grief, they inspire as well what might be called apocalyptic prudence. Deighton, for instance, reflects not on the white-faced clock's *literal* slowness, but "the slowness" with which humanity moves to realize the "peace and fruitful living" for which we hope.[18] And "Hiroshima with its clock at 8:10 brought realization that time has almost run out"; whatever is left "is very, very short." One is reminded of the famous "Doomsday Clock" on the cover of the *Bulletin of the Atomic Scientists* (and, in the present context, perhaps mindful of the memories of Hiroshima and Nagasaki embedded in that image).

All roads lead out from Hiroshima. There are located our future images of a nuclear end and of other forms of mass extermination and ecological devastation—images that have traveled everywhere, to every place. This is why, as Jonathan Schell explained in his book, *The Fate of the Earth*,

> The Hiroshima people's experience . . . is of much more than historical interest. It is a picture of what our whole world is always poised to become—a backdrop of scarcely imaginable horror lying just behind the surface of our normal life, and capable of breaking through into that normal life at any second. Whether we choose to think about it or not, it is an omnipresent, inescapable truth about our lives today that at every single moment each one of us may suddenly become the deranged mother looking for her burned child; the professor with the ball of rice in

his hand whose wife has just told him "Run away, dear!"
and died in the fires; [the neighborhood man] running back
into the firestorm; the naked man standing on the blasted
plain that was his city, holding his eyeball in his hand; or,
more likely, one of the millions of corpses.[19]

Yet, cogent though such apocalyptic prudence remains, it does not
do justice to the time, the memory, the place of Hiroshima. Just as
the place of Hiroshima will remain if nuclear weapons—and all
manifestations of mass violence—are eliminated, so too will the time
of Hiroshima continue to claim its place. It will not become less
important to remember that time. The reasons to do so extend
beyond prudence, beyond enlightened self-interest, however crucial
those components of historical memory are. For we are dealing
here with other temporal intricacies as well—intricacies that have
truly strange, even mythological, dimensions.

The time "Hiroshima" was characterized by survivors of the
bombing, or *hibakusha*, as "that day" or "that time." "That time" is
also the place of timelessness. For the historian of religion, this
cannot but evoke Mircea Eliade's noted designation of "timeless" or
mythic time as *illud tempus:* that time, the dreamtime, sacred or
primordial time. The origins of this world are *in illud tempore,* in
that time, the time of Forever.[20] This quality of time is indeed
present at times in remembrances of Hiroshima—a primordial time
of both the nuclear age and the full historical flowering of human
violence. The poet Albert Goldbarth (writing at a time of renewed
nuclear concern, the mid-1980s) returns us to archaic depths and
places of Hiroshima time in his poem, "History as Horse Light":

It ended at the time of Hiroshima. Everything
ended, the world. Though some of us didn't
know it, and kept on, like the spasms you see
in the hips of an animal—small and useless
telegraph keys—where it's stretched at the edge of the road.
But it wasn't that slow for the horse

at Hiroshima: they'll show you its shadow
burnt permanently to a wall by the blast.
Think of such light. In *Guernica*, Picasso approaches light
like that—flash—a whole horse screaming.

It began in the Paleolithic caves. Something,
someone, surely happened before that, but
whatever matters took its first idea
of its shape in those blindblack passageways.
Somebody crawled, with a raw lamp, with a wick
and its fat. Somebody made his way through
rockgut, crawling on his knees like a beast,
rising where the space permitted, making his necessary
Aurignacian way to a place where a horse could be put
on a wall in the first light's first distinctions . . .[21]

The poem leads us from the historical memory of "the time of
Hiroshima" back toward an art of protest (*Guernica*), and thence to
"blindblack" passageways of the psyche, and finally to an original
vision, a horse-memory imprinted on the wall of a primordial cave.
Now the time when "It ended" and the time when "It began" are
present at the same time (and in parallel time are Everything and
Everything's lover). The image of each time is made more vivid and
emotionally striking by its juxtaposition with the other and by the
way each evokes "timeless" time.[22] We are in many times and places
at once—recollecting Hiroshima, the place of the nuclear flash; the
luminescence of Picasso's *Guernica*; and a cave of originary light, of
first distinctions. And, in that light, an animal-ancestor of the
nuclear age, an invocative image from Stone-Age time.
    What renders this cave of origins postmodern is its tacit irony,
its juxtaposition of primal artistic creativeness and primal world-
destructiveness. Contemplating this juxtaposition, we approach the
place of the sorrow that lies beyond blame. We go the way of
"pure and imageless greases sputtering down the dark," in the words
of "History's" conclusion. The "time of Hiroshima" resolves into

and echoes all the places and times of history that have witnessed the human capacity for violence and killing in action. In this conundrum of times and places we confront the manifold destructiveness, the *inhuman* power and strangeness, of human violence—its nuclear heritage. We contemplate the impulse to create or renew worlds through cruelty and killing, and the range of our lamentation extends.

The time of Hiroshima, with all the places and images it evokes, is foundational and ever-present. Its place, though symbolically denied by the cancellation of the Smithsonian exhibit on the atomic bomb, remains with us forever. There is no way back to our origins, but perhaps we can get a glimpse of them, and make some fresh starts, by sustaining the awareness that Hiroshima is here to stay.

7

Opening Images

The cancellation of the Smithsonian exhibit, of the images of nuclear destruction, illustrates a pattern of response to Hiroshima and Nagasaki that, with few exceptions (principally eras of antinuclear feeling and activism—the years immediately following the bombings, the late fifties and early sixties, and the early to mid eighties), has characterized our relationship with nuclear images: denial, repression, and a closing-out of these images' horror and strangeness. In a word, inhospitality.

Yet the images remain, challenging us to become more open to them. Sometimes, unwittingly, we are. The attempt to shut out nuclear memories is both exemplified and undermined by the veteran's assertion quoted in the opening chapter: "The pumpkin dropped on Hiroshima and Nagasaki saved hundreds of thousands of American GIs." This seems a straightforward reiteration of ornamented and idealized history, of the need of group forgetfulness, though the euphemistic expression may function as a cover for a deeper, more discomfiting level of memory. But wait. A nuclear *pumpkin*? Think about it, imagine it. What comes to your mind? Or, if you will, what *doesn't* come to mind?

"I don't think of All Hallow's Eve," said a friend to whom I posed the question. I do—which is not surprising—but let's not jump the gun. My friend's first association, which I had not thought about, is very much to the point: he understood the pumpkin to mean the mushroom cloud. I was thinking about smashed pumpkins, about kids running riot on Halloween, about an unwitting acknowledgment of a link between violence and a certain kind of ecstasy (as well as relief) in the veteran's image—and most definitely about visitors from six feet under. I didn't at first see the pumpkin as a mushroom cloud, but there it is, a nuclear jack o'lantern.

And underneath this visage are others, which is where the older traditions associated with Halloween come in. The comments of Sir James Frazer in *The Golden Bough* are as timely as any.[1] Hallowe'en was one of "the principal fire-festivals of the Celts," and like similar festivals elsewhere that mark transitional or (to borrow the name of a Japanese Buddhist holiday) All Souls' Days, an occasion "when the souls of the departed were supposed to revisit their old homes . . ." For how "could the good-man and the good-wife deny [their hospitality] to the spirits of their dead . . .?" It is not only *their* dead that come out; "The fairies, too, are all let loose, and hobgoblins of every sort roam freely about." And though the veteran's comment expresses a wish to close out the spookier and more foreign characters, Hallowe'en is a time of openness to imagination's foreigners; "all the fairy hills are thrown wide open and the fairies swarm forth . . ." The openness of the time has its risks; one saying includes this caution: "Avoid the road children, children."

Among the descendants of these children are not only contemporary trick-or-treaters and roving gangs of pumpkin-smashers, but, to quote one title, the *Children of Hiroshima*. Another place, analogous to "the fairy hills," may open wide as well—the Memorial Mound in Hiroshima's Peace Park, in which the ashes of some 70,000 bomb victims are said to be housed. When these stranger children and Bomb People come—together with the spirits of all dead—to our doors, what sort of commemorative offering do we have for them? And how can they receive our offering if our own doors are not open?

The memorable character of images associated with "that time"—whichever of them strike your mind—is inescapable. Which is why they are emotionally striking: they are, like all souls' festivals, *openings* into worlds suffused with strangeness and death. Through psychological commemoration we can provide for ourselves a defined time and place wherein doors are opened and we may meet the images face-to-face. Having considered the psychological nature of the *place(s)* and *time(s)* of Hiroshima, let us face the images, beginning with the experiences of actual *hibakusha*, who faced them first.

Outside witnesses of the bombing of Hiroshima and Nagasaki, as well as *hibakusha*, often speak of horrifying images burned, engraved or otherwise impressed in memory, like the horse shadow "burnt permanently to a wall.". The authors of a comprehensive study of *Hiroshima and Nagasaki* say that "Certainly the most sweeping and searing destruction ever visited upon mankind left an enormous, abhorrent, and lifelong impression in the minds and memories of its victims. . . . Despite the passage of time, the memories of these survivors are strikingly vivid and concrete."[2] Robert Jay Lifton, writing of his interviews with survivors seventeen years after the bombings, remarks that "what impressed me throughout the work was the vividness of recall, the sense that the bomb was falling right there in my office—a vividness which seems to reflect both the indelible imprint of the event and its endlessly reverberating psychological repercussions."[3] One image suggesting the "indelible imprint" of the experience appears in Masuji Ibuse's novel, *Black Rain*.[4] The marks left by the "black rain" that fell from the atomic cloud upon a young woman's hands will not wash off and remain "firmly stuck on the skin." And a "reverberating" image sounds in a description of one *hibakusha's* being haunted by voices and cries of other victims at the time of the Hiroshima bombing: "Memories of 'that day' quite simply refused to be silenced."[5]

Speaking of the moment the bomb fell—of a red dragonfly, the sound of a B-29, his brother reaching out to catch the dragonfly and a flash—a boy, one of the contributors to the *Children of Hiroshima*, muses: "It is strange. These fragmentary scenes remain fixed in my mind like photographs."[6] "Even now," says a girl, "the sight of Father coming up the road toward us, his head wrapped in bandages, using his one good eye, and walking with a cane, is engraved in our memories."[7] In commenting on a picture he drew for the volume *Unforgettable Fire*, a man writes of "a charred body of a woman standing frozen in a running posture with one leg lifted and her baby tightly clutched in her arms. Who on earth could she be? This cruel sight still vividly remains in my mind."[8] Another man, who lost his own son to the bomb, tells of a "miserable image" of a junior high school boy, burned and dying as he pleads for water, which "always haunts me."[9] Psychologically, the man is perhaps "father" to this image—the image serving also as his lost son, evoking endlessly reverberating grief. In his time, and our own, miserable images continue to haunt us, to provide an opening for sorrow.

Such images, far from healing, may, in salutary ways, open and re-open our wounds. Dr. Takashi Nagai, a survivor of the Nagasaki bomb (he died in 1951), writes of himself and his fellow victims: "We carry deep in our hearts, every one of us, stubborn, unhealing wounds."[10] This can be amplified in an unexpected manner by the experience of Father Kleinsorge, who begins to feel symptoms of radiation sickness during his walk through the ruins of Hiroshima. A few days later, back at the Jesuit Novitiate outside of Hiroshima where he is staying, "the rector, who had examined Father Kleinsorge's apparently negligible but unhealed cuts daily, asked in surprise, 'What have you done to your wounds?' They had suddenly opened wider and were swollen and inflamed."[11]

Consider this opening of wounds caused by the damage done by radiation to the body's reparative capacities as an image: what are the effects of nuclear images on our psychological bodies? Opening ourselves to such images and placing them in memory will mean opening and amplifying, or *un-healing*, wounds. The soul opens wider in pain to the stubborn wounds of its heart, its tissues now "swollen and inflamed." The experiences of Father Kleinsorge—who, as a figure in the primary story of *Hiroshima,* can, like the Rev. Mr. Tanimoto, be taken as a kind of mythic character of the nuclear age—echo in us all. We who were not present at the bombings of Hiroshima and Nagasaki drink often from the safe waters of Un-Care, and have tended to consider the damage of these events to our individual and collective psychic lives as relatively superficial and minor, like Father Kleinsorge's cuts. Yet "We carry deep in our hearts, every one of us, stubborn, unhealing wounds" which are only "apparently negligible." And they will open wider and deeper when we return, like Father Kleinsorge, to the site of destruction.

The psychological commemoration of the first atomic bombings involves a therapeutic perspective in which the emphasis is less on healing and health than on the "un-healing" of the soul. Here we give open attention, and are open, to the un-healing wounds and inflamed tissues of nuclear images. Yet this practice has its prenuclear traditions: the art of memory with its disfiguring operations, the grim figurations of Dante's *Inferno,* the sometimes graphic images of flaying, dismemberment, and mortification in medieval alchemy, and the violence of religious imaginations ancient and contemporary. In this way too Hiroshima and Nagasaki reveal the past, present, and future—the soul's unceasing devotion to images strange and painful.[12] We meet with many times and places in the course of exploring the wounds of nuclear images. These all become imaginatively linked—by *psychological* connections between woundedness, openness and depth. To be wounded by images is to be "open"—so that one's depths are exposed to imagination and memory, and one's threshold becomes a place where one can meet the strange and the dead—listen to what they have to say, and offer them the commemorative hospitality that is properly theirs.

8

Psychological Commemoration: A House for Hiroshima

The psychological commemoration of Hiroshima and Nagasaki can take place vicariously and indirectly, through reading, contemplation, conversation, and public action; it doesn't require the kinds of immediate encounters portrayed below. But let's say that something in you is curious to see what—or who—might appear if you should seek a more direct meeting with characters from the first nuclear All Souls' Days. If such might be the case, one way to open-mindedly enter the place of Hiroshima would be to notice precisely what images "Hiroshima" evokes in your mind—following, in a modified way, Jung's practice of active imagination (which always begins with whatever images are present to one and follows no preconceived itinerary). Just pause and consider those images, whether they are recalled from some account (fictional or actual) of the bombings of Hiroshima and Nagasaki, or from a dream you once had concerning war or nuclear matters or, perhaps, something else that is quite personal, idiosyncratic.[1]

The images evoked by "Hiroshima" need not be literally *from* that place in order to express its psychological power. Moreover, you may notice that the images come you to already placed—or are, in effect, their own places. This initial imaginative foray can be extended in a variety of ways, leading to the kinds of encounters between habitual self and imaginal other that characterize active imagination, to the placing of images associated with Hiroshima in a classically-defined memory house, or to innumerable combinations of these forms of imaginative exploration. In any case, what is involved is the construction—or remembering—of a house for Hiroshima, a place that will abide independently of conscious, recollective memory. As in any form of all souls' observance, the openings are mutual: you imaginatively enter into places and images as you entertain them in the "house" of your psychological life. And you too see yourself (and are seen) as an image: part of you identifies with the "road children" of Halloween, or the "Walking Ghosts" filing in and out of Hiroshima and Nagasaki.

Consider the initial exploration of Sarah, a woman in her mid-thirties when I spoke with her in 1985. At the time, Sarah was politically active in nuclear disarmament and other antiwar efforts. Her fears were close to the surface. She remembered a particular dark hallway in her former elementary school; the school nurse's office opens into this hall—and the nurse may be able to provide some comfort to a terrified little girl who comes running through the hallway. Hanging on the wall next to the nurse's office door is a painting: Edvard Munch's *The Scream*. Sarah thinks also about her younger sister—ill, at the time, with leukemia. Her grief and fear have very personal ramifications. One could also find here a possible strength, in that the terrified girl evokes a capacity to nurse—a capacity that, in its own ramifications, could be present in Sarah's psychological future as well as her past.

But ramifications of the terrified girl extend far beyond the personal. A man in his sixties with whom I spoke at approximately the same time remembered, in association with images of processions of ghosts entering and leaving Hiroshima, the figure of a little girl from a photo of the Vietnam War that appeared in *Life* magazine. The girl, her face contorted by grief and panic, flees, naked, from the scene of an explosion down the road. It is this same little girl who appears, terrified and screaming, in Sarah's elementary school hallway. The distinct psychological and historical topographies of the Vietnam War and of Hiroshima become mutually evocative. And the innocent young girl who is victimized by war is a Road Child whom we meet in many places and guises as well—in Anne Frank during the Nazi Holocaust, and in Sadako Sasaki, the Hiroshima girl who died at twelve of radiation-induced leukemia.

Young female victims of war are, to our consciences, among the most "emotionally striking," highlighting with special clarity war's pointless cruelties. Then, too, the image of the innocent young-girl victim—precisely because she so frequently appears—can easily be exploited, marketed, commodified. This fate seems to have befallen Zlata Filipovic, the Sarajevan girl whose diary (*Zlata's Diary*) made the bestseller list in early 1994, and to whom the charismatic image of Anne Frank was attached. In the case of Bosnia, commercialized emotional dramatization has served as a cover for deeper despair and inaction, for the misery that, as Freud recognized, defends against profounder pain. But in this instance, too, the theme is parallel—when the innocent young girl appears, there appear as well assaultive forces, figures of estrangement. Where Persephone is, there Hades shall also be. It is this underlying estrangement that Edvard Munch so graphically portrays in the colors and contours with which he renders *The Scream*.

So there are many currents and undercurrents of the near and far, the domestic and the foreign, within Sarah's remembering of the naked little girl fleeing war in Vietnam—the girl whose terror haunts Hiroshima, the "elementary school" of the nuclear age. Hiroshima, for Sarah, can be a place as close at hand as her little sister, who suffers from the illness that remembers Sadako Sasaki. It is a kind of *migrating* place; with it, we travel to Vietnam, to the room in which Anne Frank wrote her diary, to a besieged Sarajevo, to the classical topography of Hades, and to an elementary school whose echoed halls display *The Scream*.

I stand just inside the entrance to a long stone hallway, dimly and indirectly lit, with various rooms and recesses on either side. There is the sound of a spring or fountain which I sense is near the beginning of the hallway, but cannot see. It is the House of Hiroshima, the inescapable place. The same characters are there, in the same positions that I remember from my last visit. Immediately to my left, in a recess marked by a stone archway, stands a man who is naked and has been burned featureless. Directly in front of me, on a dark green round marble pedestal, stands the charred woman clutching her baby—the "cruel sight" from Unforgettable Fire. *The mother stares straight ahead, her face burned into a mask. You see only suggestions of the whites of her eyes, the contour of her nose. But the mouth stands out—its charred lips curled back upon themselves reveal clenched teeth. Perhaps in* rigor mortis, *perhaps in rage. Perhaps this is the face of Medusa's own panic. It seems that the lips quiver slightly, if you allow yourself to contemplate this mother's face.*

Confronted by these figures, I sense a vague but oppressive suggestion of the smell of burnt and rotting flesh. I glance at the man in the left corner, who also seems vaguely to writhe in contortions of pain. The sight of him, together with the suggested odor of death, now reminds me of the victim of poison gas depicted in Wilfred Owen's searing poem protesting World War I, Dulce et Decorum Est. *The victim writhes convulsively, as I remember, in a greenish fog. He seems to struggle free of the body of the man in the corner and stumble deeper into the building. Fleetingly, I wonder if this could also be a gas chamber in Auschwitz, the so-called* anus mundi. *The people here speak through that wondering: "Welcome to the asshole of the world."*

In the place of Hiroshima, our imaginative explorations reconstitute the place of memory. The sensed placings of images, here as at the scene of the disaster that gave rise to the art of memory, are part of what makes their character "indelible." Hersey's *Hiroshima* follows this principle as its narrative weaves its way among the experiences of the six survivors chronicled.

A slightly less immediate way to imaginatively enter the place of Hiroshima is through a careful reading—or ceremonial re-reading—and contemplating of that primary text. Much can be discovered along that way, as in the case of our recognition of the person of Ferryman, who highlights a mythic theme of the nuclear age—movement toward underworlds.

Returning to *Hiroshima,* we notice other evidence of such movement. Or rather, a constant reiteration of movements, beginning with burials, descents, and movements out of consciousness or one's mind and into dark places.[2] Having first introduced us to six survivors and describing their pre-bomb locations and activities, Hersey returns to each during the moment of the explosion and the fiery devastation that immediately ensued. Terrorized by "a sheet of sun," a man with the Reverend Tanimoto "buried himself" among bedrolls while Mr. Tanimoto "threw himself between two big rocks in [a] garden." When he looked up, "Such clouds of dust had risen that there was a sort of twilight around." Looking around, he first sees "soldiers who had been burrowing into the hillside opposite," apparently to resist a possible invasion by Allied forces; now they "were coming out of the hole," dazed, silent, and wounded; meanwhile "the day grew darker and darker." Shortly thereafter, Mr. Tanimoto climbs a hillock to look out over the city below; "as much of Hiroshima as he could see was giving off a thick, dreadful miasma. Clumps of smoke, near and far, had begun to push up through the general dust." He thinks "of his wife and baby, his church, his home, his parishioners, all of them down in that awful murk."

Mrs. Hatsuyo Nakamura, in her house with her three children, is thrown into another room by the atomic blast. "Timbers fell around her as she landed, and a shower of tiles pommelled her; everything became dark, for she was buried." She frees herself and then her children—two of whose voices she hears (in what becomes for us an echo of Goldbarth's "Paleolithic caves") "from what seemed to be caverns far below . . ." Her five-year-old girl asks, "Why is it night already?"

Dr. Masakazu Fujii, relaxing in his underwear on the porch of his riverside hospital, finds himself, along with the hospital, in the river. With "his head miraculously above water," he is "squeezed tightly by two long timbers in a V across his chest, like a morsel suspended between two huge chopsticks"—as though about to be devoured by something far larger than himself. After hanging "there about twenty minutes in the darkened morning," Dr. Fujii realizes he will be submerged by the rising tide and manages to free himself. Wandering in bloody underwear, he winds up seeking refuge from fire in the water, with many others, under a nearby bridge.

Father Wilhelm Kleinsorge, the Jesuit priest, had already been under the weather before the bomb, suffering "from a rather painful and urgent diarrhea"; when the flash came, as he "later realized," he was reminded "of something he had read as a boy about a large meteor colliding with the earth. . . . Then, for a few seconds or minutes, he went out of his mind." He comes to in another world, "wandering around in the mission's vegetable garden," utterly vulnerable, "in his underwear . . . the day had turned dark . . ."

Dr. Terufumi Sasaki, in the Red Cross Hospital corridor with a blood sample in his hand, is immediately immersed in a somewhat different hell, a hospital "in horrible confusion" with dead and wounded and screaming patients and colleagues. Hersey, with implicit irony, again speaks of invasion: "all over Hiroshima, maimed and dying citizens turned their unsteady steps toward the . . . [h]ospital to begin an invasion that was to make Dr. Sasaki forget his private nightmare for a long, long time."

The fate of Miss Toshiko Sasaki, the clerk in her office, brings one of *Hiroshima's* most telling ironies to the surface. After the flash, "Everything fell, and Miss Sasaki lost consciousness" as bookcases behind her fell on top of her. "There, in the tin factory, in the first moment of the atomic age, a human being was crushed by books." After a long period of unconsciousness, Miss Sasaki becomes aware of "dreadful pain in her left leg. It was so black

under the books and debris that the borderline between awareness
and unconsciousness was fine; she apparently crossed it several
times . . ." Her person, like everyone else's, is transformed forever.
She ends up being moved under a corrugated iron sheet with "two
horribly wounded people—a woman with a whole breast sheared
off and a man whose face was all raw from a burn"; there "the
three grotesques," immobilized, remained through the day and
"began to smell quite bad."

Mourning is gravity's desire, which is why when we cease resisting
it and return to Hiroshima we can, like Jung initiating his "confrontation with the unconscious" and Brent Staples viewing the
photos of his dead brother—fall "down and down for miles."
Whether or not we make our conversations with remembered
images explicit in the active imagination Jung advocates, like Jung
we go through "a steep descent" into a "land of the dead." There
we must suffer the cries of "people buried and abandoned," as
Hersey puts it, in the decimated city. The cries of all children
prematurely "buried," in whatever ways, resound from "caverns far
below" that are also right beneath our living spaces. In such places
of far below, we wander, wounded, barefoot or in underwear,
amidst walking ghosts.

The place of Hiroshima need not, of course, be literally
imagined as an *under*world, but certain underworld qualities accrue
to it no matter where it is located or how it is imagined. As surely
as the dream that initiated psychoanalysis, Hiroshima, the initiatory
"dream" of the nuclear age, has a "navel . . . where [the place]
reaches down into the unknown." The place of Hiroshima, because
it is also placeless, reaches us wherever we are. This horizontal
reach (remember the early atomic-bomb surveyor's association of
the streets of Hiroshima with those we know as Michigan,
Constitution Avenue, and Broadway) means that Hiroshima's navel,
its vertical dimension, is likewise wherever we are. Under our feet,
over our heads. No matter how far up or down we go, Hiroshima
hangs over us and opens underneath us. Robert Lowell gives us a

memorable image of Hiroshima's inescapable binding of the foreign and domestic with the horizontal and vertical in his "For the Union Dead":

> on Boylston Street, a commercial photograph
> shows Hiroshima boiling
>
> over a Mosler Safe, the "Rock of Ages"
> that survived the blast. Space is nearer.[3]

There is a disconcerting kinship between Lowell's home city of Boston and Hiroshima which locates itself in the bond of sound linking "Boylston Street" and "Hiroshima boiling." Through his spare words Lowell brings to the fore a cauldron of images, a conjunction of particular places that evokes the falseness of nuclear "safety." There is the annihilation of memory, of permanence—the ironic "Rock of Ages"—and of all distinct earthly places. After Hiroshima, empty "Space is nearer." For "The infinity and silence of space . . . signify the absence of place."[4] Yet this near absence, this infinite above, signifies also the presence of the place of Hiroshima below, its voices calling out from beneath our own foundations, insisting on themselves, breaking the surface of silence, drawing our desire into the Unknown.

In the Unknown are the images. They may appear as alive, dying, dead, or as ghosts—or, perhaps, in between life and death, sharing in the status of the wanderers of All Souls' Anniversary. They may be well-known and actual, like Father Kleinsorge of *Hiroshima*, or unknown and fictive; more precisely, they are likely to be a combination of both. They may emerge from other sources of imagination, places of fantasy and dream and history we remember in connection with Hiroshima, as is the case with the Vietnamese girl fleeing war. Whatever their sources, we may find them altered or distorted by fantasy so as to better reflect the metaphoric psyche, as with my traveling companion whose burnt hands get me in touch with frictions in Russian-American (together with other) relationships. (There is a parallel to Dante's figures, who are modeled on historical persons but disclose and evoke other characters as well.) Whoever they are, they seek our care.

The work of psychological commemoration helps us recognize how history and fantasy are inevitably bound together yet also distinct. Keeping in mind this distinction allows us to further notice the distinct presence of each in the other. In a soulful form of commemoration, the truth and precision of fantasy is accorded a place alongside an insistence on accurate historical documentation and memory. So that when a friend of mine, on hearing of this book, thinks of terrible scenes "in the streets" right after the bomb hit Hiroshima that she remembers from the book *Hiroshima Mon Amour*, the conflation, which she quickly recognized, of the film with Hersey's account, reveals a truth. Scenes from *Hiroshima* are located in a film about unhealing wounds of love—a far-reaching, suggestive commingling. For my friend, and for us all, the place of Hiroshima may remember, may open wounds of love.

What we need, then, is a *psychological* fidelity, a careful noticing of what is present in imagination rather than a whimful constructing of images according to our usual wishes or preconceptions (historical, empirical, moral, or otherwise). But attention to literal ("factual") truth is just as important. Here, the literal and the metaphoric are not enemies; as the tacit truth of my friend's mis-remembering shows, they can distinguish and enrich each other.

If you are moved to connect with images such as have emerged here, ask yourself: What position do the characters take? What are they doing? How might you respond to their suffering? Do you (and others) seek to avoid them out of some deep dread that you might be infected with the taint, the pollution, of their suffering and death? The actual "atomic bomb people" have suffered, and continue to suffer from discrimination due to this archaic fear. Perhaps the psychic figures you meet have been avoided for a similar reason, so that their suffering is compounded by isolation. But something in us is drawn to these figures: can you feel your secret fascination with woundedness and death while moving through their places? You may be horrified, indignant, or feel guilty and desire to take on the images' suffering as your own. Something in you surely suffers *with* them, and in your compassion you may want to help or heal these figures. But perhaps—as Dante learns in the *Inferno*—there is no hope, help or healing here; and the most that can be done is to give care and attention to suffering itself, providing a place in our hearts for these cavernous open wounds.

Images conjure themselves through our bodies, as did my friend, the spirit of Hiroshima. An imaginatively embodied empathy seems necessary to the psychological commemoration of Hiroshima. As well as figuring underworld topographies of the nuclear era, John Hersey offers numerous instances of this kind of commemorative empathy in his *Hiroshima.* So let us return again to where "Wounded people supported maimed people; disfigured families leaned together."[5]

Mr. Tanimoto rescues two "badly burned" young sisters whom he finds standing in the river. Later, the younger child complains of the cold, in spite of heat of that first post-atomic night. She "had huge, raw flash burns on her body; the salt water must have been excruciatingly painful to her. She began to shiver heavily . . . she shook more and more, and said again, 'I am so cold,' and then she suddenly stopped shivering and was dead."

Though relatively unscathed himself, Mr. Tanimoto, in his capacity as Ferryman, is in intimate contact with the grotesquely wounded as he transports them on his boat. He tries to help one woman on board, "but her skin slipped off in huge, glovelike pieces." The burns of the naked people he lifts into the boat remind him of those he had seen earlier: "yellow at first, then red and swollen, with the skin sloughed off, and finally, in the evening, suppurated and smelly"; still, he lifts "the slimy living bodies," though "he had to keep consciously repeating to himself, 'These are human beings.'" For he is in touch with inhuman dread.

Hersey's tale works in part because such utterly inhuman, foreign experiences are skillfully juxtaposed with more ordinary ones with which we can readily empathize. Mr. Tanimoto, for instance, at one point trips on someone who says, "Look out! That's my hand." Being stepped on—literally and metaphorically—is something we are likely to have experienced in some fairly immediate way. Our empathetic remembering then echoes, opens, and widens, becoming an avenue to the more extreme experiences in *Hiroshima.* At the same time, if we allow those more extreme images to dwell with us—perhaps simply by meditatively attending to them for a few minutes—their bodily reverberations make contact with other, closer-to-home experiences. The travelers on the roads of Hiroshima go in all directions. That girl to whom "the salt water must have been excruciatingly painful" can come to dwell in our remembered experiences of having salt or another substance such as hydrogen peroxide come into contact with a wound or burn—or with our most severe experiences of cold. These memories in turn are placed in quite intimate, evocative regions of our personal lives. Something of Hiroshima makes contact with those regions, deep inside our houses.

During the first night of Hiroshima, we thus become able to be with Dr. Fujii as he "lay in dreadful pain throughout the night on the floor of his family's roofless house on the edge of the city"; with Dr. Sasaki as he moves "aimlessly and dully up and down the stinking corridors" of the Red Cross Hospital binding the wounded; with a colleague of Father Kleinsorge's who is being transported on a "wooden litter" which "must have been terribly painful for [him], in whose back scores of tiny particles of window glass were embedded"; and with Miss Sasaki as she spends the night "beside the woman who had lost a breast and the man whose burned face was scarcely a face anymore, . . . suffer[ing] awfully . . . from the pain in her broken leg. She did not sleep at all." For there is something in her pain, and ours, which never does sleep.

Again I return to the stone hallway; now I walk past the man
burnt featureless and the charred woman and infant on the

pedestal. To my right is a room with an open door. I look in but do not enter. The room is completely black, but flecked with stars—it is the night sky. There are stars on all sides but no one is there. Leaning into the room, I discover it is airless, for I try to draw a breath but breathe in nothing. Through that empty breath, the room comes to inhabit me. Then, just as Robert Lowell says, "space is nearer."

Diagonally across the hallway is another recess. Again, no one is there. It consists of a window with the glass blown out, framed by the tatters of a shade swaying in the wind. This place is black and white, like a movie I remember that consists of footage from Hiroshima and Nagasaki. The sky that shows through the window is cloudy and bright and vacant. The window is too high up for me to see out of, but I know that it looks out upon Hiroshima just as it was when the film was taken, a few days after the bomb. It too would be in black and white—that is, all in gray.

Deeper now into the hallway, on the other side. There is a large, white, round stone pillar, and, further to the right (or east), flows the Ota River—of Hiroshima, of "that time." A river of bodies, remembering the Kagera, flowing from Rwanda into Lake Victoria. Against this backdrop, sitting with her back against the pillar, facing toward the river, is the Girl that says, "I am so cold," and dies. This has gone on forever: the Girl says, "I am so cold" and dies. It is always the same.

It happens that I descend from a "non-combatant" in a war. But here I realize that there are none. My Uncle Lester, a soldier, was killed in Italy in World War II—a spirited guy who can never be more than a wraith in my mind. When the family received word of his death, my father says, "Your grandmother went to bed," her spirit frozen there.

The Girl in the house of Hiroshima forever says, "I am so cold," and dies.

9

Eyes of Hiroshima

There is something you will likely encounter in the place of Hiroshima that is, in its way, harder to face than the worst outrages. Nor will it comfort you much to realize that it can't be helped. But it can be faced and named; in truth, we have already done so: imagination's fascination with death, injury, deformity. What do we remember if we look more deeply into that fascination?

First, it is inseparable from the place of Hiroshima. An undertone of fascination with hideously deformed and injured figures colors much remembering and imagining of Hiroshima, Nagasaki, and potential nuclear holocaust. I believe echoes of such fascination can be heard whenever these places are invoked. Mrs. Nakamura (of *Hiroshima*), for instance, returns to the city four days after the bombing, though quite ill. For "All week, at the Novitiate [where she and Father Kleinsorge were staying at the time], she had worried about her mother, brother, and older sister, who had lived in the part of the town called Fukuro, and besides, she felt drawn by some fascination, just as Father Kleinsorge had been."[1] Dr. Michihiko Hachiya, a physician *hibakusha* and author of the seminal *Hiroshima Diary*, tells of how one man repeatedly described grotesque scenes he had witnessed. "It seemed to give [the man] some relief to pour out his terrifying experiences on us; and there was no one who would have stopped him, so fascinating was his tale of horror."[2] Yasuko, the young woman protagonist of Masuji Ibuse's novel, *Black Rain*, is, despite herself, fascinated with the horror of Hiroshima, unable to stop herself from looking at three dead women in a water tank.[3]

What is going on within this immemorial fascination with woundedness, death and pain that the images of Hiroshima force us to remember? Lifton observes that "Much of the survivor's fascination with these horrors has to do with his inner contrast between those experiencing them and himself—in the unconscious reassurance that 'they, not I, are being brutalized,'" and adds that "aggressive and perverse" fantasies may be evoked by these scenes.[4] Let us contemplate for a moment that aggression and perversion.

Julia, a woman I interviewed several years ago, vividly imagined three rooms as her "house" of nuclear images. In one room is a container filled with "melted, deformed, dripping" people and garbage; in describing it, Julia noted hesitantly that "the Christian part of me said" not to look at those things, for that would be almost "perverse." But she could acknowledge that "I wanted to see how [a particular deformed] face looked."

Part of the value within the imagination of Hiroshima is precisely that we are confronted with, must *face*, these darkly disturbing fantasies that we all can remember experiencing in some form: those characters in us who are fascinated by horror—characters we'd prefer to consign to the place of refuse or garbage container within, as Julia's image aptly puts it.

More psychological precision is needed as we face the depths of what we ordinarily refuse to look at. For these places have religious dimensions, as suggested by the inherent fascination in visions of Hell. This might be related to "the Christian part" of our culture, in Julia's image. However, there is no religion of which I'm aware that does not include, in its public ramifications, some place for cruel fascinations, punishments, deaths. The monotheistic religions can justly be criticized for fostering violent intolerance, or the infliction of hells by one group upon another. Yet even Hinduism, traditionally tolerant of differing religious paths, can take fundamentalist shape, as the recent destruction by a mob shouting "Atom bomb! Atom bomb!" of a mosque in Ayhodhya, India shows. And though not emphasized by most Buddhist practitioners, there are in Buddhism images of hell as harrowing as any. Older and polytheistic religions feature sacrifice, rape, dismemberment; the connection between *Violence and the Sacred,* as Rene Girard calls it in his book of that title, is ubiquitous.

This connection is illuminated by a more recent controversy—one that itself tellingly connects with the animosity aroused by the prospect of accurate portrayal of *others'* hells at the Smithsonian exhibit and Hiroshima Peace Museum. I'm thinking of the 1994 banning by some Islamic countries of Stephen Spielberg's film about the Nazi Holocaust, *Schindler's List,* because of its portrayal of the suffering of alien others. In a more trivial vein, some countries cited sex and nudity in the film as reasons for censorship. It happened here "at home" too: some American parents' groups objected to the showing of *Schindler's List* to high school students for the same reasons. Even if we bear in mind significant cultural differences, it may be that a focus on sex and nudity may in both cases be in part a refuge from larger anxieties and contradictions with which any remotely faithful portrayal of the Holocaust—or any agony of strangers—confronts us.

But the explicit reasons for opposition to the showing of *Schindler's List* were religious—a "Christian part" of some parents' concern in the United States, and an "Islamic part" of the reason why some countries sought censorship. Such censorship is unacceptable; we should never give in to it. But let us nevertheless consider that yes, there is a form of "sex and nudity" associated with massive and genocidal violence. Something fascinating is uncovered which literalized religious morality seeks to repress. But a death-oriented desire, as evidenced by the cruelty, the hells of religion, still manages to expose itself. Face it: religion taps humankind's most murderous potentials. What is the place of sadism within the religious spirit?

Perhaps that place needn't be seen through literal and polarized lenses only. Perhaps, if it always does, as I believe, claim some place, then it is that place which asks our metaphoric concentration, our commemoration. For fascination with death and with images in deepest pain, though it may always have some literal *potential*, need not be literally acted out, visited upon actual others. And we can turn our question about religion's cruel fascinations on its head and elaborate: does our late twentieth century "love of the grotesque" disclose hidden possibilities of religious imagination, of a different kind of love, of devotion to what is painful, than is evidenced by the violence—the acted-out ideologies of apartness—of history's inquisitions and of contemporary religious extremists of whatever creed? To try and answer this question at this juncture would be premature, but what is apparent now is that *the place of Hiroshima is a place of religious cruelty*; and it is an immemorial religious cruelty that we remember in granting Hiroshima its place. The question must be posed—it wounds us and, in the process, opens new metaphoric possibilities. But if we try too quickly to answer it, we might then be able to sidestep additional questions posed by religious cruelty—questions of guilt. Guilt fired by the presence of impulses we can't help.

Crucial to Lifton's masterful portrayal of the psychic turmoil suffered by Hiroshima survivors is its exploration of death guilt. For "survival, by definition, involves a sequence in which one person dies sooner than another, [so] this struggle in turn concerns issues of *comparative death-timing*." Guilt arises "over survival priority, along with the survivor's unconscious sense of an organic social balance which makes him feel that his survival was purchased at the cost of another's."[5] If fascination with dead and pained others involves an element of self-reassurance, it inevitably provokes guilt—hence also a feeling of connectedness with those others. Within cruel fascinations lie complex combinations of separation from, and connection with, those beyond ourselves. Parts of *our*selves are pained, wounded, killed, wrenched from our usual sense of self-identity, ferried to an estranged shore. Death guilt is not literal only, but becomes a metaphoric vessel of passage. We can't help but mourn when we meditatively face our fascinated demons. But in so doing, we can begin to see ourselves also through the eyes of others.

Let us then look more closely at (through) these eyes of others. One of the more haunting themes in the survivor psychology of Hiroshima is the persistent sense that one is being stared at accusingly by the eyes of the wounded and dead. This both echoes and provokes self-condemnation and death guilt. Mr. Tanimoto is thus haunted. In Asano Park, he encounters his next-door neighbor, a mother, holding her dead infant daughter. She asks Mr. Tanimoto to try and find her husband, whom he is fairly certain has been killed, so that the husband can look once more at their daughter. Mr. Tanimoto knows he will fail. And from then on, while in the park "he always felt he was being watched by" his neighbor. For "whenever he looked at her, she was staring at him and her eyes asked the same question." It is the question of guilt, for to survive in the place of Hiroshima is to fail others.

Again, a history professor describes walking through the ruins of Hiroshima looking for his family, "looking carefully at everyone I met . . . the eyes—the emptiness—the helpless expression—were something I will never forget. . . . There were hundreds of people who had seen me. . . . They looked at me with great expectation, staring right through me. It was very hard to be stared at by those eyes . . ."[6] Memory and guilt are kept vividly alive—along with the images of the dying and dead, the pained and the helpless—by these eyes through which one is seen, and from which one's own eyes cannot turn.

The themes of guilty fascination, looking, seeing, and being seen dovetail in the experience of Dr. Hachiya. He relates a tale told by a visitor: "Well, I saw a man whose eye had been torn out by an injury, and there he stood with the eye resting in the palm of his hand." And "What made my blood run cold was that it looked like the eye was staring at me. Doctor, the pupil looked right at me. Do you think the eye could see me?"[7]

The visitor's image soon becomes a visitation, a presence within Dr. Hachiya's psychological vision. In his entry of 23 August, he records a discussion with another doctor who ran the Eye Clinic at the Communications Hospital, concerning the blinding burns to the eyes received by many who had looked at the nuclear flash. The following night, says Dr. Hachiya, "I slept poorly and had a frightful dream."[8]

> It seems I was in Tokyo after the great earthquake and around me were decomposing bodies heaped in piles, all of whom were looking right at me. I saw an eye sitting on the palm of a girl's hand. Suddenly it turned and leaped into the sky and then came flying back towards me, so that, looking up, I could see a great bare eyeball, bigger than life, hovering over my head, staring point blank at me. I was powerless to move.

Awakening from this nightmare, Dr. Hachiya, thinking that the visitor's story had been "too much" for him, lies in bed and worries about an inability to remember names of acquaintances and friends "since the *pika* [flash]." This "blindness for names" leads in turn to worries about whether his own eyes may somehow have been indirectly damaged by the *pika.* "Maybe my eye nerves were weakened by the *pika.* I could not believe I had retrograde amnesia. Can one get an optic amnesia?"

Before and after the nightmare, Dr. Hachiya's thoughts and ruminations revolve around blindness and forgetfulness. The nightmare, by startling contrast, presents a horrible vision of total and unforgettable seeing: together with the dead, the *dreamer* is seen and remembered. All the dead look right at the dreamer (note the implied psychological identification of dreamer and the waking visitor); the dreamer watches an eye, "bigger than life," leap up and stare down at him, rendering him "powerless to move." The dreamer is thus fixed in memory by the Eye(s) of the Dead, rendered as a static memory image. He will not be forgotten.

Dr. Hachiya's ruminations surely express his individual psychic struggles, his contradictory impulses to be blind to the horror of his world, to forget what he has seen (also his sense that, by virtue of surviving, he has in fact been blinded to and forgotten the dead), and his need to see and remember—all of which impulses express and provoke death guilt.

But the dream, as the nightmare of *Hiroshima Diary*, is also a primary nightmare of the world's nuclear imagination. As Richard Rhodes puts it in his chronicle of *The Making of the Atomic Bomb*, "the dream of this Japanese doctor who was wounded in the world's first atomic bombing and who ministered to hundreds of victims must be counted one of the millennial visions of mankind . . ."[9] Let us probe the *vision* of this dream more closely. The unforgettable image of the man holding his eyeball having penetrated the consciousness of Dr. Hachiya, the dreamer is placed, "It seems . . . in Tokyo after the great earthquake [of September 1, 1923] . . ." That disaster and the one in Hiroshima are condensed, so that Hiroshima becomes a kind of Tokyo or capital of the country after the earth-shaking horror of the atomic bombing. There are probable allusions to the entire Pacific War and the great upheaval of Japan and its heart or "capital" that occasioned the rising militarism and nationalism of the earlier twentieth century.[10] And an *earthquake* is also a notable underworld image; the residents of Kobe and L.A. will testify to that.

Because Hiroshima is an end-of-the-world time, and because a capital city in nationalistic or other group-centered cosmologies connotes the center of the world, the dream can also be seen to imagine the earthquake at the heart of the larger nuclear world. By speaking in the image of Tokyo after the great earthquake, the dream seems to stress these cultural and cosmic themes, and its way of combining them may paradoxically represent a move toward the de-centering of group identity, a move away from an "us/them" psychology. In its guilt-provoking eyes we glimpse the deeper remembrance of Hiroshima that could catalyze, in Japanese political conversation, a more profoundly mournful remembrance of Japan's wartime cruelties, and, ultimately, a movement into the realm of sorrow beyond blame. But, just as Kobe speaks to L.A., the dream speaks to all who experience ideologies of apartness.

The images of the multitudinous eyes of the dead and of the "great bare eyeball" that flies up to look down upon the dreamer, are worth still closer attention. Jung, in his researches into the psychological patterns within alchemical images, found numerous examples of sparks, stars, and eyes that suggest our awareness of consciousness and subjectivity beyond ourselves. For instance, one symbol "shows eyes in the stars, in the clouds, in the water and in the earth," and one religiously-oriented alchemist says of heaven that: "It is like an eye and a seeing of the soul, whereby the state of the soul and her intentions are made known to us."[11] Marsilio Ficino (who advises us to house the universe in our dwellings) likens stars to eyes as well.[12]

So too that house I enter, with its tormented characters who seem to place me in a position like Dr. Hachiya's—whom I look at, fascinated, in spite of myself. Remember the room I have to face—the one with its staring stars. Remember the eyes of the mother, staring me down each time I enter her house, penetrating my image of myself.

In Dr. Hachiya's dream (as we all are) the "helpless" eyes of others become the powerful ones, while the dreamer is powerless, a motionless memory image. "Bigger than life," the detached eye it has a life of its own, having been torn from the human context; flying up from the dream-girl's hand—as though in shamanistic ecstasy—it stares down from above (like "eyes" of heaven). It is now a *higher* eye.

Eyeball-Man (as we may call him), in the dream-context of *Hiroshima Diary*, appears then as an inescapable presence in the world of "after-the-bomb." *Hiroshima Diary*, written by an early medical researcher of the effects of nuclear weapons, records the world's beginning awareness of nuclear actualities. In remembering eye-images we focus on the psychological background not only of guilty self-scrutiny, but more generally of research and in-sight into the nuclear world. In a number of ways, Eyeball-Man and Dr. Hachiya's dream embody possibilities of postnuclear self-examination. The images we face are all eyes as they decompose themselves and reveal the de-composure of our selves, together with our group-centered identities, in this house of dying and remembering. This post-Hiroshima consciousness is multiple, torn and scattered in inhuman death, and unnerving in the intensity of its presence. By these images that are eyes we are seen, our guilty fascinations remembered. Remembered in magnified form—under the microscope of Hiroshima.

In this remembering, much is deformed, let go, forgotten. What is forgotten and disfigured above all is our habit of identifying ourselves in terms of ideologies of apartness: self vs. not-self. Instead, we cultivate multiple images of self and not-self and part-self, images that are always multifaceted combinations of selves and others, images that ferry us among and within multiple worlds. The movement begins with desire flowing in the direction of dead, injured, pained others, proceeds to guilt-infused self-scrutiny, and then to a relativizing and multiplication of one's self-image—the revisioning and reconstituting of collaborations between familiars and foreigners. It is in this process of mourning and loss that Hiroshima is realized as a place of psychological commemoration, of pained intricacy, of blame-wounding sorrow.

Different images carry and implicate (hence allowing us to apprehend and discern) numerous emotional and affective qualities. An image may embody terror and panic, deep and gentle compassion, a slow and melancholy endurance of unendurable torment, bitter rage at the violence and horror of history. These places and images are indeed "emotionally striking": sheltered in the house of Hiroshima are unfathomed hate, loneliness, wonder; eyes flashing, tearful, vacant; hands reaching, stroking, miming the world's dance of pain. Not only do we come to know the images present; we are also known by them. They each have their own perspective, their own specific way of remembering—remembering ourselves, remembering the world. This is an occasion for us as well: an occasion to sense how the world might be remembered in a way quite different from what we *ourselves*, apart from these images, could ever imagine.

I stand again before Who-on-Earth. For that seems the proper name for the charred woman and child on the deep green marble pedestal, regarding whom another Hiroshima survivor wonders: "Who on earth could she be? This cruel sight still vividly remains in my mind." Hiroshima Man, with the skin dangling from his fingers, stands with me. To him, the rage and grief of Who-on-Earth is palpable, throbbing through his hands. I notice now how she glowers in our direction, her eyes blazing. I think fleetingly of a picture I saw in a 1993 newspaper, of a Bosnian citizen glowering at a U.N. relief official, making the motion of slitting the throat with her hand. I am acutely uncomfortable that Who-on-Earth is on a pedestal; I don't want her to be there. But I can't help it, and there she remains. Does she remind me of murderous rage that I myself could feel but may instead condemn in others?

Yes, sometimes such rage quickens within me because I hold in my hands graphic despair—a charred image of the future. What do I look like from Who-on-Earth's point of view? I feel myself shifting slightly in my discomfort—like the man burnt featureless who still stands in the recess to my left. Why must such suffering and such rage be on a pedestal? How do I grasp the tendency to exhibit pain and rage and death? How do I face it in myself? Like Who-on-Earth, it is finally unidentifiable, that which remains when fixed identity has become unrecognizable. But fixed identity's decimation claims a place of display.

Springs well up in the eyes of Hiroshima; fountains set his burnt and lacerated face afire. At once forgetting his wounds and whelmed by all they transmit to him, Hiroshima reaches out to gently touch Who-on-Earth's right cheek, as if to infuse her with his life. He reaches out of a sense of curiosity as well, but the curiosity, I realize, is mine, not his. To my surprise, Who-on-Earth seems to smile slightly, and I'm reminded, at that moment, of the smile of the Mona Lisa.

II

THE MOURNING OF ECOLOGY

10

The Trees of Hiroshima [1]

Just before embarking on this book (in early March of 1994), I had a frightening and confusing dream in which

> *a ship runs aground off a city in Norway—some kind of military transport vessel. Its crew exits the ship, and then I am in the city's downtown sector and a nuclear attack begins. There are multiple, blinding explosions. I watch, horrified, as buildings are reduced before my eyes to piles of rubble from which blackened beams protrude. People on the streets try desperately to flee.*

I awakened from the dream to discover that the image that most sticks in my memory is that of the blackened beams protruding from the rubble. Somehow, their starkness is especially frightening. It moves me to think of other scenes of destruction—scenes I had witnessed, and scenes recalled to me by others. Especially, I begin to think of the destruction of forests. For instance, as part of a study of the psychological importance of trees and forests, I traveled to the Charleston, South Carolina area after Hurricane Hugo in the fall of 1989, and to South Florida after Hurricane Andrew in the fall of 1992 to speak with local residents. [1] To the

north of Charleston lies the Francis Marion National Forest, which
has large tracts of loblolly and longleaf pines planted for timber
harvesting. The scene there reminded me of blast-bent smokestacks,
of tropical forest devastated during the Vietnam War—and, most
disturbingly, the bombed cities of Hiroshima and Nagasaki.

These memories helped me to think about the dream's "military
transport vessel." For, as I found in talking with people in hurricane zones, military devastation often transports itself in our
imaginations to scenes of devastated nature. A number of South
Carolinians saw in the devastated Francis Marion a "war zone," the
horror of "'Nam" (as one woman put it), or of other bombed-out
places. One man, thinking of barrier islands that had been virtually
flattened by the wind and accompanying storm tide, spoke of a
place that "looks like I would think an area would look like in the
vicinity of a nuclear explosion. Of course I've never seen one, hope
I never do."

This is not so unusual. As Elias Canetti observes in his study
of *Crowds and Power,* the forest has historically been seen as
analogous to the army; metaphors of burning forests and falling
trees—from the *Iliad* to Stephen Crane's *Red Badge of Courage* and
twentieth-century poetry expressing nuclear fear—lie ready to hand.
There may be special significance in such transport of military
characters to places of ecological loss, ecologies of mourning. The
military itself functions in many cultures as a form of *initiatory
transport vessel,* a rite of passage into adulthood through realms of
death, a ferrying power. But perhaps one needn't literally and
actually enter the military in order to be transported, somehow
initiated, by military imaginations.

My particular psychological makeup leaves me especially
vulnerable to repeated "initiations" of this sort, periods of pain and
dread occasioned by episodes of needless violence and threat. When
the military vessel runs aground, the spirit of Hiroshima suffers
further chafe and jar. But this is not only a personal affair. For
images of military destruction ground themselves near shores of the
soul, come to grief there. And then they can become vessels of
transport into awareness of loss and deepened ecological concern.

To state it in a way that exposes the main idea of this chapter: when humankind's military vessels run aground, the mourning of ecology can begin.

A citizen of a contemporary Balkan nation tells us: "the land remembers . . ." Its features figure dreamtimes, historic and prehistoric. Experiences of ecological loss (whatever the cause) put us in touch with land that remembers, as illustrated by the recollections of three people from the Homestead area of South Florida with whom I spoke after Hurricane Andrew: they made explicit analogies between what Andrew had done and the destruction of Hiroshima and Nagasaki. One thought of "nuclear explosions . . . and Hiroshima"; another, a retired military man, remarked: "I've been to Nagasaki and Hiroshima; I've seen what we can do, and like I say, it's very similar. . . ." A third, speaking about the tropical botanical garden where he worked, described the scene there in images that I believe my dream remembers. What he saw the morning after Andrew was "what I imagine a bomb dropping would be like. After seeing scenes of Hiroshima and Nagasaki—just the profile of the skyline, with trees barren of leaves and just the sticks . . . just the limbs sticking up in the air . . ."

There, I believe, are the blackened beams of my dream's Norway city—its most impressive, sticking images. In them we have examples of the interplay between images connected with Hiroshima and Nagasaki on the one hand, and ecological loss on the other. The man who spoke of "the sticks" also thought of Andrew's devastation as a figure of human-created devastation of tropical forests, whose diversity was represented at the botanical garden. But I had not dreamed in the tropics—why Norway?

In August of 1992 I visited Moscow for the first time. I was surprised to see what appeared to be the same kind of maple trees that are widely planted on streets and lawns in the Northeastern United States. That made it seem more like home. But the maples to which I'm referring are native not to the United States, but to northwestern Eurasia. In the States, we call them Norway maples.

In Moscow, I was close to their original neighborhood, and they made me feel somewhat at home. They are foreign here, and while commonly planted and quite graceful, they're not entirely welcome, since they compete with native species and damage local forest ecosystems. I share in this feeling to some extent, partly because of my special love for the indigenous sugar maple (a tree threatened by a combination of blight and acid precipitation). Still, in the woodscapes of my own biography, particular Norway maples in my neighborhoods have been important to me; I remember them intimately, as friends. Growing outside my windows, they offered me views of leaves when I needed them.

Norway maples bring to mind various frictions between foreign and familiar that the spirit of Hiroshima feels so acutely. Shortly after my "military transport vessel" dream, I dreamt that *the leaves had returned. I was in the woods and the trees had leafed out. What especially stood out were Norway maple saplings and seedlings, whose leaves were just shy of their full reach.* Other dreams of Norway maples followed, as though to insist that these trees harbor still more memories. And that, I realized, they do.

For one thing, I am a Norway maple. My family's roots are in Russia; we transplanted to the United States around 1900. Like all immigrants, we were not entirely welcome, were seen by some as weed trees. We came to this country in part to escape bigotry (in the form of Russian anti-Semitism), but bigotry, as a manifestation of the forgetfulness of group memory, is found to at least some degree wherever people have taken hold. The bigotry I've encountered has never been that severe, but, as a Norway maple, I remain aware of being different. I'm a bit shy—always, it seems, just shy of some fuller reach. My relatively dark complexion, wiry dark hair, and long-limbed nose make me recognizable as a transplanted species. When I was a child, others would sometimes ask me what seemed questions both curious and not entirely sympathetic, like, "Are you Italian? Are you part Negro?" (Ironically, when living in New York City, I was several times asked by Arab cab drivers if I was from "the Middle East," the evident sympathy of their question implying the hope that I was a fellow Norway maple.) When I visited Russia, I carried with me a mingling of hope, excitement, and anxiety, since we were Norway maples even before our family left Russia. I did not have any evident experiences in Russia of anti-Semitism, though Russian friends there made clear that it remains widespread, and that the difficult conditions in Russia provide it fertile soil.

One hospitable Moscow cab driver, it is true, would seem to have inadvertently alluded to my Norway mapleness. As we passed by a statue of Alexandr Pushkin, he commented to me that my features reminded him of Pushkin's. It happens that "our greatest poet," in the words of one Russian friend, was partly of African descent. (Ralph Ellison's insight about all American citizens being "somehow black" applies in some sense also to Russians.) Pushkin, the pre-eminent African-Russian, was a Norway maple.

The spirits of Hiroshima and Nagasaki are also Norway maples, but—like us others—not entirely analogous to those who colonize and disturb ecosystems. As these spirits take hold, they do disturb, but in a way that helps protect ecosystem integrity. The deeply disturbing stories they commemorate and evoke help rouse the resistance of place to devastation. As the trees of Hiroshima migrate, they spread seeds of mourning and ecology.

In this regard, I also associate Norway with ecological aware-ness—with the deep ecology of Arne Naess, about whose work I had been reading shortly before my initiating dream. Of course Norway isn't "purely" ecological; I think too of the country's role in the controversy over whaling. Yet there are in Norway potent sources of that current in ecological thought which most empha-sizes the intrinsic value of beings not human. Nor do I think this unrelated to Norway's role in the rescue of Jews during the Nazi Holocaust. For while ecological concern and racism can and do co-exist, I do not believe that apart from a more thought-out—more mournful *and* more celebratory—ecology, we shall truly find refuge from bigotry, which refuge is basic to ecosystem integrity.

Norway, moreover, happens to be the last place I visited during a summer in Europe in 1977, when I was a college sophomore. I thought it one of the most beautiful. I traveled with a couple of companions I met on my trip, going north of the Arctic Circle to view the midnight sun from a perch one thousand feet above an ice-choked lake. Traveling south, we met up with fjords (resonant with films I subsequently saw of the topography around Hiroshima) and forests. One of the latter, in the mountains above the city of Bergen on the southwest coast, was, due to its exposure to moisture from ocean winds, peculiarly lush—almost a rainforest. I took photos but don't need to look at them to remember that rainy, fern-bedecked forest of conifers and hardwoods, including maples.

From that foreign, familiar place I carried with me memories that have gone on ramifying, as they do in my above dream. A few years later, I put together a slide presentation on the psychology of nuclear threat and disarmament. Included were photographs from Hiroshima and Nagasaki after the bombing, showing mangled structures and dead trees. One of these I captioned with T. S. Eliot's words from *The Wasteland:* "where . . . the dead tree gives no shelter." Against this backdrop images of the Norway forest stood out as particularly persuasive advocates for preservation of nuclear peace. So, toward the end of my slide show, I inserted what I thought was my best picture of that forest—its trees looming in fog, beckoning, I hoped, to the viewer. I did not know then how unoriginal my idea was.

In *Hiroshima,* John Hersey recounts for us the first time in the nuclear age that people's imaginations moved them in the direction of refuge among trees. "All day, people poured into Asano Park," the place we have identified as the "safe place" of death. Traditional topographies of death often include woodlands; so too *Hiroshima.* The park, a private estate,

> was far enough away from the explosion so that its bamboos, pines, laurel, and maples were still alive [by this point the reader has passed by defoliated trees with charred

trunks], and the green place invited refugees—partly because they believed that if the Americans came back, they would bomb only buildings; partly because the foliage seemed a center of coolness and life, and the estate's exquisitely precise gardens, with their quiet pools and arching bridges, were very Japanese, normal, secure; and also partly (according to some who were there) because of an irresistible, atavistic urge to hide under leaves.[2]

This "irresistible, atavistic urge" is also given testimony in Alexander Deighton's observational aside: "in the public parks great numbers of both wounded and dead were congregated."[3] And again, in Nagasaki. There, according to Tatsuichiro Akizuki, the wounded and dying converged on a thickly-wooded hill, "where several kinds of oak grew," and it is "among the trees" of the place that a husband and wife took shelter.[4] In Akizuki's and Hersey's accounts, the trees stand out—are specifically named.

The trees are named as well in a surprised journalist's reflection on people's responses to the decimated landscape of Homestead, Florida, after Hurricane Andrew:

It was the trees that so many people spoke of.

In the midst of the devastation, the privations and the pain, the people of Homestead last week sometimes stopped, mid-conversation, and remarked on a pine tree that had grown up with them, an acacia that was a benchmark for their lives, a towering mangrove that was a testament to their own struggles, achievements and now loss.

They spoke of the scent of the leaves, the shape of a particular trunk or crown, the shade from the burning South Florida sun and the stretches of green that had made Homestead special.[5]

The post-Andrew longing for leaves may echo the desire for the shelter of trees after the atomic bombings. That idea is less far-fetched than it might seem, for painful situations incline both individuals and groups to seek solace and solidarity amidst trees—on this point, there is evidence in scientific studies, clinical observations, literature, poetry, and individual anecdotes.[5] In the nineteenth century, that inclination took the form of the construction of greenhouses in oppressive urban areas. In the decades after the bombings of Hiroshima and Nagasaki, it took the form of well-designed and wooded peace parks in those cities. But the way had been prepared by people's responses in the immediate aftermath of the bombings—and by something that inspired hope among Hiroshima residents in April of 1946: near the town hall "two cherry trees . . . blackened by the explosion" bestirred themselves; "white blossoms suddenly appeared on the charred branches and thousands flocked to see them."[6] In the mid and late 1980s, against a backdrop of global nuclear threats, there was again a turn toward arboreal shelters. This movement took the form of concern about destruction of tropical rainforests, but also bespoke a pained desire for contact with trees themselves (revealingly, the South Carolina man and South Florida gardener quoted before mentioned imperiled tropical forests immediately after referring to nuclear explosions).

It is that same ancient longing that I felt in putting together my slide show; and it is a similar urge, I believe, which in connection with nuclear threat has helped energize ecological concern since Hiroshima. The forest preservation (and restoration) movement of the 1980s has grown to include old-growth forests of all kinds, and has also ramified into innovative approaches to urban and community forestry, all of which in some sense take after the peace parks of Hiroshima and Nagasaki.

The pattern we follow in this movement, like so many others that can be associated with the place of Hiroshima, contains echoes of many times, prehistoric and historic. To some small but significant degree, the ghosts of those who fled to the still-living trees of Hiroshima are remembered in contemporary concern for forests. This too provides an opportunity for commemoration—commemoration of an avowedly ecological nature.

In the end, we shall have to go still more deeply into the Asano Park of August 6, 1945. For the moment we remain in its neighborhood, where we can experience and contemplate the ecological longing that drew so many victims of the Hiroshima bombing. We have yet to fully appreciate why that particular place and time—the morning of the atomic bomb and its location in Hersey's *Hiroshima*—is also an early morning time of the ecological imagination.

The neighborhood we are in impels us to stay with trees. For trees are agents of memory, places of commingling of human and others. There is in us a particular kinship with trees, an intimacy that comes from their presence in us as fellow upright living beings—beings who, in fact, provided us shelter during the long period of our evolution into a kind of life that mimes the trees' own way of standing. Yet our "animal mobility" (in Edward Casey's phrase from the epigraph to this book) defines our concurrent differences from trees—and therefore our yearning for roots, for the kind of intimate attachment to place which trees alone enjoy. It is because we are both different from, and parallel to, trees, that we seek and celebrate the treelike. Trees are primal places and images of memory, and every image of memory, especially those purposefully and imaginatively placed—indoors, outdoors, and in-between—takes treelike hold in us and leafs out into the future.

That is why the urge stirred by the living trees of Asano Park—and, by implication, all trees of the nuclear age—can be recognized as evolutionary. That is also why, in so many tales, the massive death of trees evokes the massive death of human beings—and why tree-planting often figures so vitally in the ecology of mourning. Consider this memory image:

On the left, inside the gate of the cemetery, stood a forest of stone. Each monument was carved in the shape of a tree trunk with its branches lopped off at the base, like a torso without arms and legs. The monuments were of all different sizes, each with its own unique shape. The effect was

grisly. I looked at the inscriptions, commemorating the
185,000 Jews from [areas in Romania] massacred [during
World War II by pro-Nazi Romanian soldiers]. Each
monument stood for a particular town or village.[7]

The narrator, Robert D. Kaplan, is writing from the vantage-point
of 1990 in Romania; an old Jewish man has taken him to this
forest. The deformed, uniquely-shaped torsos of trees become
emotionally striking memory images evocative of horrors present
and future as well as past: the Nazi Holocaust, the genocidal war
in Bosnia which was ongoing when Kaplan's book was published,
and the devastation of actual forests. The reader of Kaplan's
account is likely to remember on some level all of these, and thus
to commingle humanitarian with ecological feeling. The monuments themselves—petrified tree torsos standing for particular
human communities—are a manifestation of this commingling.

Implicit in such densely-forested historical remembering is also
our prehistoric link with trees. This link can by itself prompt
historical remembering, as in the case of those for whom Hurricane
Andrew's devastation brought to mind Hiroshima and Nagasaki.
And it can prompt ecological remembering—a remembering of
inhuman, prehistoric time—as in the case of those who fled to
Asano Park. Or, echoing Goldbarth's cave of memory ("History as
Horse Light"), it may mingle human and nonhuman memory, as in
the case of a Hiroshima writer who recalled: "there was a fearful
silence which made one feel that all people and all trees and
vegetation were dead."[8]

11

Questioning Identity

All people and all trees and vegetation dead: this leveling image marks
the decimation of distinction. It is an image that poses a topical
question—that of how we make distinctions in the first place. We
tend to conflate human distinctiveness with identity, but recently
questions have arisen regarding the very notion of identity, its
tendency to posit an absolutized, literalized, and incommensurable
difference between groups and individuals. For it is, ultimately,
some form of identity to which all victims of mass violence are
sacrificed; identity, our image of Hiroshima suggests, ultimately
obliterates distinction, kills it off. Identity, I would argue, presupposes an ideology of apartness; and such an ideology psychologically kills off true distinctness, leveling everything truly individual,
and confining memory within the province of collective self-
commemoration. Moreover, identity as a specifically *human*
construct at least tacitly segregates us from the rest of nature. There
is, psychologically, a well-traveled avenue leading from the leveling
of people, trees, and vegetation in Hiroshima to our contemporary
violence against people, trees, vegetation, and just about everything
else.

Keeping Hiroshima in mind, listen to Nelson Mandela speaking
of the idea "that the welfare of every individual and population

group could best be developed within its own national community."[1] This is perhaps the basic idea behind "identity politics," which, as we've observed, has in the past decade been linked mainly with left-oriented movements in the United States and abroad. But Mandela is paraphrasing the 1959 words of an Afrikaner government official who is attempting to justify the arbitrary subdividing of South Africa. The architects of apartheid sought "to restore power to traditional and mainly conservative ethnic leaders in order to perpetuate ethnic differences that were beginning to erode"—the consequences of which included the violence between members of the Zulu Inkatha Party and African National Congress before Mandela's election as president. In truth, the Afrikaner Nationalists were acting on the notion "that whites had an inherent right to take measure to preserve their own identity as a separate community," and "Apartheid was designed to divide racial groups," to keep them from working together. Designed, that is, to promote group self-commemoration and its corrosive forgetfulness.

If we are serious about working together, about shaping a planetary culture of nonviolence, we will, I believe, have to sacrifice not only our privileged identities, but the very notion of identity itself. I mean human identity in all its forms—individual, group, and species. Tellingly, trees and vegetation and other "ultrahuman" beings (as philosopher Neil Evernden aptly calls them) do not, strictly speaking, have identities.[2] They are distinguishable; they have identifiable characteristics, what Evernden calls "wild otherness," even a kind of subjectivity or personality. But we cannot say they have identities, for to have an identity implies a self-conscious, *oppositional* awareness of difference between self and other. And such a polarized awareness tends, as Hiroshima says, toward the obliteration of all distinctions—all forms, all places.

Further exploration of ecology and mourning (and what takes place in psychological commemoration) might help us find languages of (individual and cultural or group) self-definition not based on the rhetoric of identity. Such ways of speaking will not rest on ideologies of apartness, nor posit an Us and a Them, for they have no need of enemies. As philosophers Julia Kristeva and Jacques Derrida would say, this means recognizing "otherness" in ourselves and articulating "differences without opposition." But first we must ascertain how the leveling image of Hiroshima has been remembered (or acted-out) of late in the search for identity.

The assumed need of identity has contributed much, over the past decade, led to the progressive stultification of American social-change movements lamented at the start of this book—their fragmentation into mutually exclusive groups each centered on its own pain and renewal, its own egoism of victimization, to the exclusion of others and of the planet itself. This is reflected in the recent exclusion of concerns about continuing dangers posed by nuclear weapons and other fundamentally ecological threats from recent political discourse; it is identity that eclipses the planetary imagination.

Ironically, it may be a planetary anxiety that has fueled the retreat of political imagination into identity problems—and contributed to the recent neglect of planetwide dilemmas. This retreat started, I sense, on about June 13, 1982. June 13, 1982 was the day after a million people rallied in New York's Central Park for a nuclear freeze. The nuclear freeze movement started losing steam right after the rally, and the expression of nuclear dread was progressively less often tolerated. Our culture's more usual denial of nuclear anxiety reasserted itself. Increasingly, when I brought up nuclear threat or other ecological issues in groups working for social change, I was impatiently told to confine my focus to "real people's" immediate oppressive circumstances. Anything else was dismissed as "romantic," "unrealistic." I was criticized for emphasizing "ideas and not people," as one colleague put it, the implication being that I was too fortunate a gentleman to understand the realities of oppressed people's workaday lives. How could I presume to speak meaningfully to the experience of those not in my assigned category of identity (white male intellectual).

I am not alone when I say these experiences could make me feel a bit like Simonides, who is ostracized for commemorating outsiders, and like Decimus, whose treasonous stance toward convention marks him for punishment. Except insofar as the trends toward apartness among social-change and environmental movements, together with associated academics and theories, resulted in a diverse community of the alone, of the cut-off.

Like right-wing movements, progressive movements based (whether tacitly or explicitly) on identity politics suffer imaginative and spiritual shutting-down. But it is right-wing movements that have been most often able to turn this psychological failure into sociopolitical success. Through adroit use of the media, through deft manipulation of people's pain and anxiety in the face of uncertain futures, right-wing identity politics has in the past few years achieved stunning electoral success: for instance, in Russia in late 1993 and in Italy and the United States in 1994. (The removal of the memory of Hiroshima from the Smithsonian represents another political victory for right-wing identity politics.) Its success has reached genocidal proportions in places like Rwanda and Bosnia. These movements more starkly act out the eclipse of the planet—and of all conversation and hospitality.

Identity politics ultimately stifles freedom of imagination and of compassion, which is why its true beneficiaries are reactionary and authoritarian movements. Its egoism of victimization is a form of execution—an extirpation of the marginalized. A monument to selective self-commemoration, to the forgetting of the sufferings of others, to the denial of more encompassing sources of hope that focus less on the specialness of particular groups, and more on the particularities of the special planet that we share. Focusing on identity (from the Latin *idem* "the same"), seeking only commemoration of the same self at the banquet, we stay in the position of Scopas, forgetting the collapse that can take place any time now. In truth it already has. Hiroshima being forever, it always is, and always will be.

Ecological concern and awareness, being vessels for the memories of the first atomic bombings, may offer a way out of the collapsing confines of self-commemoration. Consider, for instance, something upon which the language of identity, regardless of group-specific idiom, relies: the search for *roots*. Though issues of identity and of cultural roots are usually framed in exclusively human terms, the language of identity still relies on a nonhuman image that evokes, however indirectly, the trees in which our prehuman forebears made their homes. Our diverse human languages do not consist solely of a din of disparate babblings; trees, animals, mountains, oceans, and others form an intelligible part of their deep structures.

Recent psychological work emphasizes the possibility of empathetic identification with the natural world (a world inclusive of human and nonhuman beings). Such identification is, in fact, woven into our human self-images. If we define ourselves as human only, we do ourselves and the world a disservice. But our imaginations nonetheless know better. When we speak the language of identity, with its emphasis on finding (or returning to) roots, we simultaneously talk the talk of trees. The emphasis on human identity so stunts our imaginations, however, that we delude ourselves into thinking we can only speak one language at a time—and into considering that language intrinsically more valuable than all others.

Still, we talk the talk of trees. But can we walk their walk? That depends on if we are able to put ourselves in their shoes. And that, in turn, depends on our being *psychologically* able to put ourselves in more than one place and more than one form at a time. To be able to imaginatively place oneself in the places of others (and give others a place in our own places) is crucial to our capacities for empathy, for larger identification. And identification places us outside any single or fixed identity, even when we feel more connected to some forms of cultural affiliation than to others. In this, we can identify the spirit of John Keats, who wrote in a letter that a poet like himself is a "chameleon" and "has no Identity—he is continually in for—and filling some other Body . . ."[3] Walking the walk of others—trees, fellow humans and other animals, mountains, oceans, sky, planet—radically expands our capacities for self-definition. Identity loses its privilege—becomes a role or set of roles we play, an always provisional part of our self-definitions.

Once identity has lost its privilege, we can inquire more deeply into its particular illusions. Identity is no essential structure—as Erik Erikson implies it is when he defines "ego identity" as "the accrued confidence that the inner sameness and continuity prepared in the past [through childhood personality development] are matched by the sameness and continuity of one's meaning for others, as evidenced in the tangible promise of a 'career.'"[4] That Erikson relates identity to *career* is of interest. This definition sounds suspiciously like Jung's concept of the *persona*, "a complicated system of relations between the individual consciousness and society, . . . a kind of mask" having to do first and foremost with one's work role(s).[5] So that a parson, a cobbler, or a poet (Jung's examples) must "play the part assigned to him"—and no other, since the parts are conceived as mutually exclusive. Career, identity, and persona coalesce along the lines of a polarized perspective. Thus the "sameness and continuity" of Eriksonian identity also have their counterpart in the Jungian persona; one would not want to be *both* a poet and a cobbler, "because society is persuaded that only the cobbler who is not a poet can make workmanlike shoes." (How ironic that most poets also wear other hats—as in T. S. Eliot the banker and William Carlos Williams the doctor—working unlikely jobs to put food on the table.) Better "present an unequivocal face to the world" than be thought "odd" or "different." In the process, the equivocal intricacy of one's individuality is compromised, and for that reason Jung repeatedly warns against identification with the persona, a one-dimensional self-image. Questioning identity, recognizing it as a *role*, is a way of heeding Jung's warning.

Yet, though Jung acknowledges this but rarely, the persona can be something more than a necessary evil, a compromised formation. For our (not only human) surroundings help shape the roles—and there are many—through which we face the world. In his 1925 lectures, Jung defines the persona in a way that differs revealingly from his above definition: "a system of relationships . . . whereby I am never apart from the effect of the object on me."[6] We are never apart from the effects of others on ourselves—this is the unremarked ecological core of Jung's image of the persona. It requires extension beyond the human sphere, into the realm of the multispeciated invocative images of myth. Keeping identity in question allows us increasingly to define ourselves—our styles and the consistencies in our ways of being in the world—by the ramifying ways in which we identify with others. Those ways of identification—to be sharply distinguished from blind identification with a single social identity—can also shape the roles we play, and enhance (rather than vitiate) our sense of individuality.

The distinctions among *self-definition, identity, and empathetic identification* are elusive, but can be more plainly stated in the language of trees, as the following encounters will show. The first involves Dave, a South Carolina man whom I interviewed three months after his home was smashed by Hurricane Hugo in 1989. Dave was in serious psychic pain as a result of his ordeal. But, oddly, our conversation reached a high point when he reminisced about an old dead live oak tree on his (former) property. He had "just left it" standing there, he said, suddenly perking up.

Noting Dave's new aliveness, I asked him why he had done so. "Well," he replied, "[I] saw no reason to do anything other than that, for one reason. And, you know, birds perched in it, it provided some foraging for woodpeckers. . . . And I saw no reason to remove it. And that's the type of individual I am." Dave spoke with a conviction that revealed his identification with this particular, highly regarded dead—yet life-supporting—tree. In identifying with it—and with those the tree supports—he defines who he is and asserts his self-integrity, an integrity inclusive of life and death, ecology and mourning.

Dave's dead live oak exemplifies how identification with ultrahuman beings can shape one's individual self-definition. An encounter with Les, whom I met while traveling in Russia in 1993, exemplifies how such beings can quicken one's capacity for empathetic hospitality—toward humans and others.

My meeting with Les took place at a conference on the possibilities for spiritual, cultural, and ecological renewal in the post-Soviet era, which took place during a two-week cruise on the Volga River. A slightly-built, middle-aged man, Les didn't show much interest in talking with the American conference participants, though he did make a critical remark about American habits to one of them. He espoused rather narrowly traditionalist views that struck others as chauvinistic. I made no attempts to speak with him during the conference because I thought he wouldn't listen, that he spoke only the language of identity. Two minutes before I had to leave to catch my plane home, I realized my mistake.

The evening before, I'd given a talk on the importance of trees in the cultural, artistic, and spiritual creativity of individuals and communities in different parts of the world. As an illustration I exhibited and discussed a photograph, taken by a fellow conference participant, of an old orthodox church framed by a wizened linden tree leaning at a forty-five degree angle over a field of snow. The tree seemed to embody the photographer's perception of the damage done to Russian spiritual life in the Soviet era, and his hopes that it would somehow muddle through, like the linden.

At six o'clock the following morning I stood on the dock at which the ship had berthed, the after-effects of a vodka-inspirited farewell gathering hanging over me. Les appeared on the deck above. We found ourselves waving goodbye to each other, though we had never met. And then, to my astonishment, Les, whom I had not seen in the audience during my talk, told me that what had been said was important and invited me up for a drink.

When I explained that I had to leave, Les struggled for words. "My English is very poor," he said, but "me and my friends like trees." He seemed, by his invitation and the words he struggled for, to suggest that he and I, too, might be friends—for friends like trees. As I walked toward a waiting commuter ferry, Les stood on the deck, his hand raised, calling out his goodbye: *Da svidania! Da svidania! Da svidania!*

Les (and the trees) showed a capacity for change and hospitality that I had wrongly assumed did not exist. My error showed my capacity to fall into unthinking assumptions about others. It was the talk of trees that broke through language barriers—less the barriers between Russian and English than those put up by the all-too-common language of identity. The trees made possible a shift from preoccupation with identity (in my case, my fixed assumptions about the immovable character of Les's identity) to an empathetic identification between strangers. They reminded me that, like ecosystems that maintain their integrity while remaining porous to other regions and planetary influences, our differences needn't be seen in opposition.

Now let's revisit Decimus, who further illuminates the relationship between self-definition and the impress of others. Decimus is identified not by what group he belongs to but by where he is—in the tenth place in a house of memory. As noted before, Decimus's image indirectly evokes memories of decimation—of pain, punishment, devastation. Also of treason. This last is most timely, for by throwing identity into question, psychological commemoration commits treason against its imperial design.

Sticking with our treasonous image, we uncover further linkages—linkages between the ecologies of loss and of place. Since the number ten symbolically evokes the completion or culmination of a cycle or process, the *tenth* place can also be imagined as the last place in a series, a final place or place of completion. Another way of imagining it is to say that place itself is what marks or completes a character or image—that place is the ultimate shaping power. Decimus has, in Keatsian terms, no identity; his shape is defined by the poetic body of his environment. He and that body empathetically flow into and mark each other's features. He assumes a persona, a mask, shaped by the place in which he stands—becomes, as it were, its spirit. Through him, one can identify, and identify with, the place(s) where one is. Decimus, with his *ecological* markings and intimations of loss, stands at the nexus of ecology and mourning. That stance is treasonous to the Roman empire of identity, which wars with others—including the souls of the natural world—as a way of cancelling out the desire to mourn.

What we might call the *ecology of identification*—particular patterns, porous placial boundaries—leads us to parallel Keats's view of identity with Buddhism's view of the self: it is ultimately nonexistent, has no actual place. It is nonexistent because there is no true ecology of identity, because identity represents the illusion of ideologies of apartness, of nonporous boundaries. The absolutized borders of identity preclude identification, preclude ecology. For identity is too pure to mix or mingle with others. A truer, more porous particularity celebrates inward differences and allows (to note one illustration) for the bold inclusiveness of Walt Whitman's identification of himself: "Do I contradict myself?/Very well then . . . . I contradict myself," for "I contain multitudes."[7] He is that kind of a place, that is, which has room for the multitudinous. And this allows for discrimination *with*—a discriminating imagination that incorporates and promotes identification and conversation with others.

Discrimination *against* others involves, in contrast, a non-discriminating imagination: discriminatory clichés and stereotypes are generalized, non-particular. In that lack of discernment of particularity the inherent brutality of identity, its *imposition of generalizations and denial of contradictoriness,* stands revealed. The illusion of identity easily takes on delusional elements in the context of collective enemy-making. Such enemy-making is precisely a form of social delusion, a radical and absolutized disjunction between one's perception and the raw experience of one's enemy other. Yet the similarities in enemies' behavior toward each other, as well as in mutually-held stereotypes, show what Jungian psychologists have identified as a form of negative identity or attribution of one's shadow side to the other. It is a negative identity that binds American and Japanese groups who have worked to suppress historical truths of World War II, even as each group seeks to maintain its own unique and pure selfhood.

When the experience of contradiction can be sustained,

identification—the imaginative commemoration of others—flourishes. And then we realize: identity is dead. Yet the dead presence of identity as a *place-making power* is necessary to the ecology of identification, allowing us to distinguish identification and relatedness from fusion or merger. Identification, like memory, like mourning, presupposes separateness and separation—distinct places and images whose characters can be remembered by distinct others. Identification calls upon our capacity to move between places, to psychologically be in more than one place at a time, to imaginatively put ourselves in the place(s) of another. And here we can recognize, even commemorate, the role that identity, now a shade of itself, still has to play in the world's dramas—dispersed, decimated, disfigured, transfigured into the capacity for identification and (following Jung's persona) the medium of relatedness. And of love of wild otherness.

The *cross-cutting connections* (and these, psychologists note, energize intergroup cooperation) provided by place and by the natural world—their capacity to serve, like Les's trees, as meeting-places—make possible the peaceable co-existence of multiple qualities and characters, or, as Robert Jay Lifton puts it, the protean self.[8] Our art of memory becomes, to appropriate a metaphor used by Cornel West, a "jazz" of memory, what West (echoing Lifton's description) calls "an improvisational mode of protean, fluid, and flexible dispositions toward reality suspicious of 'either/or' viewpoints, dogmatic pronouncements, or supremacist ideologies."[9]

But though Lifton's description of the protean self is cogent as far as it goes, it has limits. Those very limits, however, show us the rest of the way toward the replacement of identity's self-commemoration with a more imaginative, celebratory commemoration of the world—of the place(s) of ecology.

Lifton's portrayal of Proteus, the "Old Man of the Sea," does not fully consider the sea God's actual nature. Proteus is more elusive than any human self—because he is not a human being. In the *Odyssey*, Proteus appears in sequence as a lion, a dragon (*drakōn*, a fantasy creature, distinct in Epic Greek from *ophis* "serpent"), a leopard, a massive boar, languidly flowing water, and a lush tall tree. This sequence, which can be taken as an illustration of the art of memory in practice, reveals the soul of the sea, its shifting and elusive qualities. Yet it takes place in terrestrial settings. Even the image of languidly flowing water (*hugron hudōr*) is not clearly an image of ocean. Yet the sequence as a whole expresses the imaginative ecology of ocean waters, their aural as well as visual qualities (the roar of lion and leopard, the hiss of a dragon, the clamorous approach of a boar, the murmur of water, the rustling leaves of a tree). The spirit of the sea inheres in the fauna, flora, and geological formations of the land—both fantastic (dragon-like) and actual.

Insofar as this same spirit inheres as well in the human imagination, that imagination takes on ultrahuman qualities. Only by fully acknowledging these qualities—the place and presence of the other-than-human within the human resiliency and fragility of which Lifton speaks—can we be true to the sea. The problem with a human-centered psychology, or one which takes a nonhuman pattern or character as its starting-point for an exploration of the *human* self, is that it tends toward an insidious form of reduction-ism—a reduction of the ultrahuman world into a mere allegory for the human. It remains confined, even if only implicitly, within the illusory realm of human identity; and this is the case, as Edward Emery points out, with the concept of the (human) protean self.[10] However well-intentioned, such a human-centered psychology lacks a larger ecological viability, awareness, or reference point. It therefore works against our capacity to celebrate the greater natural world for its own sake, to honor and explore how we are shaped by that world, and to empathetically identify with its inhuman places, images, and powers.

The original Greek tellers of the *Odyssey* did not intend to honor the human self only, or even primarily. The *archaic* Greek imagination is more about the acknowledgment and celebration of the ultrahuman. A human-centered protean self is more in line with a later tradition—that of Protagoras, who asserts that "Man is the measure of all things." Proteus, by contrast, asserts that movement forward requires "a fitting sacrifice" to the Gods. And the *Odyssey's* description of Proteus celebrates, before anything or anyone else, the imaginative, occasionally fantastic, powers of the actual sea.

To return, then, to the larger-than-human ecological context. We know the sea is the source of life. What Proteus knows through his images is that the sea spirit seeks expression in terrestrial forms, in fact requires those forms for its realization. Here is a source of difference without opposition, of self-definition that depends on empathetic identification with images in many places—a definition that cannot be realized if confined to one proper, pure, and literal place. The sea spirit can only become itself by eluding literal identity and evoking memories of many places.

What Proteus tells us, through his various guises, is that the sea becomes itself most fully in becoming other at the same time. We, who harbor oceans of places within ourselves, can learn from this spirit about human becoming. We are neither truly human or humane if we see ourselves as human only. Not only are we inescapably linked with the larger natural world; its forms inhere in us as shaping powers of imagination. Likewise, we are seas flowing into other forms and other places; psychologically, the process of empathetic identification consists precisely in this flowing-into-others. Proteus cannot be truly who the ocean is until inspired to take on other shapes. Nor can we be truly human without breaking through the limits of human identity, finding out who the other powers of the planet are, and experiencing their passions. Including, foremost, the quintessentially protean power of place.

I now stand before the man from Unforgettable Fire *who is haunted by the dying boy whose cries for water echo the father's grief for his own son, killed in the bombing. In order to get to the father I have to go past the man burned feature-less, Who-on-Earth, the room of the Night Sky, the window in the film taken from inside the bomb-damaged building, and the girl sitting against a pillar who says, "I am so cold," and dies. Walking on the same side of the hallway, I then encounter a parade of Walking Ghosts going in the other direction—a procession of bomb victims with their original wounds, passing in silence through this place. Then, I come to a semi-dark corridor on the right; and there, opposite the corner, is the man who grieves for his lost son. I feel a piercing sadness as I look at the man, whose head remains bowed in grief. He is wearing a traditional Japanese-style robe, but at the same time, draped over his shoulders is a tallith or fringed prayer-shawl traditionally worn by Jews when praying. It is like the one worn by the rabbi of the synagogue I attended as a boy.*

"But this is bizarre," I catch myself thinking. Still, the figure before me, however strange or incongruous, is who this man really is. He has a Japanese visage, is a survivor of the Hiroshima bomb, and his head is bowed in what I now realize is a kind of "religious sadness." And he is wearing a tallith, for his sadness is also a prayer, and it must not be forgotten. I am reminded of the stench that confronts me as I enter the place of Hiroshima, how it remembers the gas chamber. Before this grief, I am forced to consider again my relationship to my Jewish heritage. Roughly since the time of my bar mitzvah, my orientation has been avowedly nontraditional—secular in a Jewish way, you might say. Nor do I now feel any impulsion toward returning to Jewish religious practice, as have some of my friends. Also, I remain critical of the tendency among some Jews to incorporate the Nazi Holocaust into a definition of Jewish identity. As a remembering of one's own group coupled with the exclusion of others, this has always felt wrong to me. Yet I celebrate and draw upon Judaism's imaginative thought and prophetic self-questioning. And I can never escape my feelings of grief, my remembering fears, which arise from the Holocaust.

I ponder now that semidark hallway at the threshold of which I find myself. I sense it as the house of all that is unanswerable and unresolvable. It is, in the image arising from the one-hundred-year-old dream of that religiously secular Jew, Sigmund Freud, the navel of the dream I now inhabit. It is the point where the suffering of the unresolvable is felt also as inexhaustible depth, as affirmation of the future, as wonder.

The way Jewish heritage finds a place in me is now through this place, the place of Hiroshima that expresses the ecology of mourning. The man with his head bowed in grief: he brings together the Judaism with which I am familiar and from which I am estranged, with the Japanese religious sensibility—which is in different ways familiar to me and strange. There is a peculiarly haunting sadness in the Japanese feeling for natural beauty that seems to coincide in this man with the sadness inherent in the contemporary Jewish outlook on history and human loss. Mourning and sadness become here a crucial meeting-place for different traditions. A place of emergence for new images that might wound our notions of what religious tradition consists of, and give more place to the other-than-human beings of the planet. Perhaps I will learn from the grieving rabbi how to make of my sadness a prayer.

Remember with me the low wooded mountain that faces the east window of my study. That mountain, my friend, has its own reply to the leveled image of Hiroshima over which we've been laboring.

The time of this writing is two days after the season's first snowfall. Though only a few inches fell and it's been relatively mild since then, here in the foothills of the Berkshires the snow clings tenaciously to the land. Together with the afternoon sun, I look out over the mountain's face. I find that, covered with snow, the land stands revealed in a way it wasn't before. Below the mountain's crown of hemlocks and white pines, through stands of bared oak, birch, and beech, I now see various wrinkles in the land which give shape to its rocky ledges. Ragged lines traverse its steep slopes—odd cracked smiles of the mountain. It is a mountain I can better relate to now. I can identify with it, think like it, because I can more precisely and carefully imagine and remember its face's impressive features.

But I would not know the mountain in the way that I do now without the help of snow. The land had to become something other than itself in order to become itself, to communicate itself. Its character was simultaneously covered and uncovered by the new snow. It has become a more memorable place, more completely expressed itself. Its deciduous trees' branches stand out as well against the snow. And I myself, together with the ways I remember and imagine, am changed, however modestly or imperceptibly, by the character of the mountain. By the sea as well—the mountain's true source of snow. The mountain's face is defined because it is able to be a particular meeting-place, a place in which the foreign and familiar can come together and not be in opposition. It lacks fixed or permanent identity but is identifiable; the different character of snow—not just any snow but *this* snow, this lingering first snow—is the means by which the mountain gets itself across in the way it does just now, during this afternoon.

12

Thinking Like Asano Park

Memories sprout from land like trees, branching out in variegations of the future. Thus the place of Hiroshima remembers itself in the experience of ecological loss, as do the dreamtime powers of Australian land when their human offspring return to them. The memories of land—our rooted attachments to place—can take many shapes. Including, sadly, ethnic vengefulness, which is the sentiment behind the assertion quoted earlier that "the land remembers." What the person was saying was that in the aftermath of ethnic killing "the land remembers every [victim], even the murdered unborn babies who have no names."[1] We have considered this as the egoism of victimization, the confinement of memory to one's own group's sufferings. Now, with the mourning of ecology in mind, we can glimpse caverns far below whose presence, if attended to, may help undermine the more superficial rhetoric of enmity. For there is another level of speaking going on here—underneath group hatreds "the land remembers" in a more salutary way. Underlying group identities and their (at least) potential hatreds may be a profounder sense of ecological loss, of severance from place. Acknowledging this loss may be essential to renewed remembrance of place, and those avenues by which place can connect us and our differences.

Aldo Leopold, one of the twentieth century's major ecological thinkers—whose persona has already appeared in my allusion, at the conclusion of the last chapter, to his celebrated essay on "Thinking Like a Mountain,"—emphasizes elsewhere that land, considered ecologically, "is not merely soil. It is a fountain of energy flowing through a circuit of soils, plants, and animals. Food chains are the living channels which conduct energy upward. Death and decay return it to the soil."[2] Just as land is more than soil, our ethical relationship to land is not merely utilitarian or economic. "It is inconceivable to me," he writes, "that an ethical relation to land can exist without love, respect, and admiration for land, and a high regard for its value. By 'value' I of course mean something far broader than mere economic value. I mean value in the philosophical sense. Perhaps the most serious obstacle impeding the evolution of a land ethic is the fact that our educational and economic system is headed away from, rather than toward, an intense consciousness of land."

With this "intense consciousness of land" in mind, consider once more Hiroshima's Asano Park. Remember that, in addition to the desire for refuge amidst foliage, Hersey observes that the estate's exquisitely precise gardens, with their quiet pools and arching bridges, were very Japanese, normal, secure . . ." In the *exquisite precision* is the power and particularity of place. In that sense, the remembering of place, whose obliteration Hiroshima arouses, started on the morning of August 6, 1945.

Yet an element of national and ethnic awareness remains: Asano Park as "very Japanese, normal, secure . . ." Normality and security—the desire for those qualities (however differently defined by groups) is common to every ethnic and national or religious particularity. It is when collective desires for secure normality—identity, in other words—begin to exclude the foreign (in contrast to what happened in Asano Park), we encounter sources of our most massive violence. Then soil is bloodied.

Leopold is uneasily aware of the blood-and-soil connection. He acknowledges another form of "intense consciousness of land" when he refers to Daniel Boone's "dark and bloody ground" in Kentucky.[3] This form of land-consciousness is vividly illustrated in a blood-and-soil story about an encounter with a party of Native Americans in Davey Crockett's fictionalized almanac. When Crockett meets the other men he mows them down (so he says) with his 12-foot scythe, as though they're crops, until "the red nigger's sap both watered and manured my field, till it war as red an striped, as Uncle Sam's flag." "Thar's a stack o'thar bones standing in the medow to this very day . . . an from the large majority o'thar blood that watered it all, I have had a treble crop o' the tallest injun grass every summer." Illustrated here is a troublesome habit in American culture—a quest for "communion with nature through conquest."[4]

But this fatal communion is hardly limited to American shores; it is present whenever a group seeks normality and security through appropriation of place and of land. And, as Davey Crockett's image of "the red nigger" and contemporary fascisms of every sort (and Japanese and German racism during World War II) illustrate, bigotry of some kind is central to such communion. For unless a foreign element can be excluded from the group, that group's unique rapport with land, with nature, with memory, seems lost. Here is a communion grounded in literalized, fixed hate. A security that, true to its roots (*se cura* "without care"), has at its perimeter a river of carelessness. The humanity of inhabitants on the other side vanishes in fields of forgetfulness. And, though this type of "intense consciousness of land" may be rationalized as an intensified remembering and honoring of the soil itself, it is actually a form of human self-commemoration through violence.

James Hillman observes that the art of memory is "a moral activity of the soul. Learning and remembering served psyche."[5] The art of memory links the powers of imagination with moral activity and concern. Psychological commemoration similarly bridges intense moral concern and our awareness of the deep pain of images, so that we can empathetically remember those others whom the polarized ideologies of blood-and-soil would annihilate. This opens into remembrance of a place whose bounds, like Hiroshima's, include us all: the place of religious cruelty.

It was after World War I and the development of his cancer of the jaw that Freud began to speak of a movement in the psyche toward death. What he later says can be located in the neighborhood of religious cruelty, where it suggests that acknowledging psychological movement toward death may be necessary on several levels. Freud reflects on sadism, masochism and aggression in his *New Introductory Lectures*: "We are led to the view that masochism is older than sadism, and that sadism is the destructive instinct directed outwards, thus acquiring the characteristic of aggressiveness."[6] For masochism has the more primary relation with the desire for death. Freud continues:

> And now we are struck by the significance of the possibility that the aggressiveness may not be able to find satisfaction in the external world because it comes up against real obstacles. If this happens, it will perhaps retreat and increase the amount of self-destructiveness holding sway in the interior. . . . Impeded aggressiveness seems to involve a grave injury. It really seems as though it is necessary for us to destroy some other thing or person in order not to destroy ourselves, in order to guard against the impulsion of self-destruction. A sad disclosure indeed for the moralist!

Let us, however, turn Freud's "sad disclosure" on its head. It may be that grave injury to the soul, and most of all to its *identity*, is exactly what's necessary to impede outward aggressiveness—if, that is, the injury can be rendered into a purposeful sacrifice, an enactment of mourning: a sacrifice that helps desacralize violence.

It is that grave and necessary injury, that religious cruelty that allows for loving devotion to images in depths of pain, to which we attend when we imaginatively commemorate Hiroshima. Needed aggressive and perverse fantasies are called forth by the presence of those images. Yes, there is a sexuality and nudity connected with our vast violence—an unbearable exposure, ravaged by censored desire. Conversely, the "grave injury" of impeded aggression opens us to foreign desire—and desire for the foreign. No wonder the imaginative commemoration of outsiders is, from a militaristic perspective, treasonous. For—yes—it attunes us to the desire of others. We enter then Hiroshima My Love.

Our grave injury points toward the perversion of mass violence itself. I don't mean that mass violence is perverse; it is entirely normal. Rather, mass violence needs to be perverted, twisted, deformed into other things. This perverting process is humane because it is aggressive to violence. And it is polymorphous. For through such perversion, "wounded" and opened by images in pain, the soul opens in empathy and compassion to the multitudinous others. Our location in Hiroshima opens the way for the incorporation of the presences of others *within* the place of one's individual psyche; *place is made for the others.* This prepares the way for identification with others, for their implacement within the places of oneself, the places of memory.

Contemplated imaginatively, images of death, separation, disintegration, woundedness, and immobility thus become sources of psychological and moral reflection. Located in Hiroshima, we meet the deaths of the cultural habits that underlie mass violence and ecological destruction in all their forms. Here, the *territorial imperatives* of the authoritarian personality and group identity give way to deeper loves of land, inflicting grave injuries on militarism and doing great cruelty to our massive violence. Ideologies of apartness disintegrate into polymorphous images. The single visions of group chauvinisms disintegrate, leaving us with the love of particular places. And this allows for a more pacific joining of our "atavistic urges" with future-affirming ecological passion. Then we can join in earnest in the work of planetary ecological restoration and the cultivation of new forms of friendship—friendship between humans as individuals and as collectivities, and between humans and those nonhuman others in whose special places we also dwell. And we find ourselves, then, acting on the basis of the commemorative reverence on behalf of which Leopold's "intense consciousness of land" speaks.

In the last chapter we considered how the ecology of place itself, taken in relation to mourning, suggests how psychological commemoration can encourage the displacement of illusory group boundaries by the deeper consciousness of land. We are now better positioned to explore how directing our attention and our love toward place's own spirit and needs can occasion the meeting of this deeper awareness of the ultrahuman with commemoration of human outsiders (the men Davey Crockett labeled "red niggers," for instance) whose spilled blood the land also remembers.

Remember that we found Saturn, governor of melancholy, at work in as the boundary-making power of place, and hence in the remembering of places for images (chapter 4, pp. 59–60). This power evidences itself in Brent Staples's concentration upon place which he describes after evoking the renewal of mourning for his brother, as it does at the outset of Hersey's *Hiroshima*. Saturn can also be imagined as the power infusing group identity and its discontents. For in mythology Saturn devours his own children in order to prevent them from overthrowing his rule. He is, or tends to become, an authoritarian personality, narrowly focused on a single vision, defensive, paranoid. He seeks familiar surroundings—normal, secure. His borders function to keep "out" (in the guise of external and literal enemies) what is really an "inner" death and sadness and strangeness.

Which again suggests that a preoccupation with identity functions to keep out loss, to impede mourning. And mourning requires a place. Which suggests that identity's preoccupation with territory conceals but also reveals a search for a place for mourning—an attempt to place loss while cloaking it in ornamented history. And this suggests the possibility of a homeopathic cure for the illusions of place-based self-commemoration, an opportunity to quicken a common love of the distinctness of place that, through its very commonality, would undermine the illusions and human-centeredness of group self-preoccupation. In this place we meet again—with Decimus's treasonous character.

Let us then attune our metaphoric ears to what E. V. Walter calls "the rhetoric of place" itself, and further explore the assault on place itself that Hiroshima reveals.[7] For the loss of place looms large in the ecology of our mourning.

The obliteration of place—or its reduction into "site"—has a cultural history that predates Hiroshima. And Hiroshima itself can function as a metaphor for the blinding rapidity of social and cultural, economic and ecological displacement that characterizes our planetary predicament. In part, this is related to our culture's technological advances, though it may also have to do with what Edward Casey identifies as the prehistoric estrangement from place inherent in our "animal mobility." James Oglivy sees an overall loss of the sense of place in "the demise of the story-teller," a carrier of precisely "localized" communal as well as private experience.[8] For contemporary culture is characterized by a

> disintegration of the near/far structure of human experi-
> ence. As travel becomes trivial the odyssey is no longer
> suitable subject matter for a story. The equalization of the
> near and the far accomplished by high-speed transpor-
> tation—which is not to be reduced to a species of commu-
> nication—renders the entire phenomenon of *locality* less
> significant and hence less a source of sharing than it once
> was. When local lore gives way to the abstract grid [or map
> of sites] of the real-estate developer the loss includes more
> than the land. The very vocabulary of intersubjective
> experience is semantically grounded in a sense of *place*
> which, once destroyed, leaves the language of intersub-
> jectivity impoverished.

Oglivy is speaking, I believe, of the *bounded* character of place, upon which the distinction between "near" and "far," this world and that, is based. It is not only travel that too often becomes trivial, but the making and crossing of boundaries of imagination and story. Flying from place to place (whether metaphorically or in actual fact), we may forget the primordial power associated with border-crossings—the power to which Ferryman, crossing the river of Hiroshima, pays heed. Jacques Derrida similarly points to the danger of that "techno-media power" which "would control and standardize" via "mobile, omnipresent, and extremely rapid media networks, . . . immediately crossing every border,"[9] constituting, as it were, a new form of transregional pollution, a kind of spiritual Hiroshima or Chernobyl. We (if we are among not those affected by *actual* nuclear radiation or other post-industrial toxicities that violate our cellular borders) often forget that land remembers. If we are in addition a member of an oppressed, marginalized, displaced community, we may struggle harder to remember place, and meet with more difficulty in doing so. Global climatic upheaval may, however, effectively marginalize and displace us all.

The decimation of place, and consequent struggles toward its reconstitution, are also *ideas* freighted with philosophical memory. Edward Casey historically locates the destruction of the sense of place in Western thought, singling out first the Cartesian and post-Cartesian reduction of particularized place to generalized three-dimensional space which, because it abstracts from and lacks all qualities of unique places, "means no place at all."[10] He then observes that the "internal" sense of time—not the *placed* time of memory explored in this essay—has been considered, by Kant and others, as more fundamental in human experience than amorphous space. Thus, "place has been doubly displaced since Descartes—first by space of a universal sort that has no place for local place, and then by time, which since Kant and the Romantics has overtaken space itself as having the privileged position."

The world of Hiroshima and after—of planetary pollution and ecological destruction, of social displacement, of global economies and communications—discloses something terrifying about this development which "means no place at all." The most revealing comment by Descartes in this regard is quoted, interestingly, by Joel Kovel in a book written in the early 1980s on "the state of nuclear terror." Kovel considers the contribution of the Cartesian division of self and nature to the nuclear terror. Descartes concludes during his *Discourse on Method* that: "I was a substance whose whole essence or nature consists only in thinking, and which, that it may exist, has need of no place."[11] Descartes thus isolates human identity in its purest form. That form of identity which "has need of no place" is what comes to fruition in the place of Hiroshima. And we've been on roads that lead from Hiroshima to our planet's every overtaxed, punished, and decimated place.

Now the value of what we have remembered in nationalism—the rhetoric of place—becomes evident. Menaced by—and mourning—the loss of place—the resurgence of nationalistic and other group-specific preoccupations is an attempt at securing, in however crudely literalized form, a place in which existence can be founded. It is an attempt to counter an unease that is at its heart ecological as well as social. The search for *literal* and exclusive identity ironically seeks implacement of what has no need of place (but not of *transfigured* identity, the place-making power that arises out of the collapse of constrictive self-commemoration). It enmeshes us in a self-contradictory attempt at a cure for our ills.

For, as Edward Casey asserts (*contra* Descartes), "To be is to be bounded by place, limited by it."[12] Psychological commemoration, through its engagement with the powers of places and images, helps us remember the being of place. And "it is in place," writes Casey, "that we are beside ourselves . . . [in place] we emerge into a larger world of burgeoning experience, not only by ourselves but with others."[13] Which means that in place, literalized images of the self are displaced—displaced by empathetic identification with others, in *their* places.

Empathy, crucially, is itself a form of place-image, deriving as it does from the Greek *en* "in" and *pathēs* "passion, emotion, suffering." To be in a state of empathy means to suffer the passion of another, which means also the passion of a different place.

Empathy means to be placed *within* a passionate state—such a state being its own kind of place, not a disembodied or abstract emotional space. In this sense, the psychology of empathy *is* the ecology of place, which has challenging implications. For it means we suffer the passions of places, that, Decimus-like, the spirits of places shape our experiences and self-definitions. Only by recognizing this inherent *ultrahuman* dimension of empathy—its place dimension—can the empathetic identification I advocate be humanely realized. For then we recognize, even revel in, the freedom of imagination to displace itself, to flow Proteus-like into many places simultaneously, rather than remain stuck in a literal fixation on one place, which is likely to lead to attempts to literally displace others.

The commemoration of Hiroshima, the distinct place of placelessness, addresses an area of crucial cultural need: that of the re-construction of the memory and imagination of place, the *de-struction* of which we have seen to be fundamental to the nuclear terror and to our Cartesian human identities. This remembering of place is revealed to us through the forgetting of group egoisms and identities of all kinds, and itself reveals a deep resistance to the nuclear (or any form of) obliteration of places that are treasured, loved and inhabited. It contributes to an aesthetic sensitivity to place in general, or to what E. V. Walter calls "making, keeping and dwelling in good places."[14] It is no pure coincidence that "unlike most of Japan's largest cities, . . . which seem to have developed without any overall sense of planning since the war, the central part of Hiroshima . . . still retains much of the character of the pre-war city"; that its "essential shape . . . has been preserved, as has the uninterrupted view of the mountains to the north."[15]

Think again about Asano Park. What kind of place is it? While characteristically Japanese, it also has another persona—that of No One's Land. The ancient desire it catalyzed moves among many places, beginning with the stirring cherry trees and reforested peace parks of Hiroshima and Nagasaki. It is a place of *commemoration through reforestation and, more generally, environmental pro-*

tection and restoration. Let the souls of Asano Park take their place planetwide.

Like all forms of No One's Land, Asano Park is not only a self-consistent place, but one that borders all places, a place where all particular places meet each other. It is the porous boundary of the place of Hiroshima, a place between worlds or All Souls' Place. It can't be found on a map, but it is where we are. Remember that Casey, in distinguishing between place and site, observes that the arbitrary grids of maps define the latter, but the former always escape them. Now, in the more elusive language of place boundaries in the natural world, we will be able to hear echoes of the spirit and nature of Asano Park. Peter Sauer, an environmental writer, tells of his difficulties in squaring an abstract "habitat diagram" with his lived experience of a given landscape.[16] For "habitats are relatively easy to identify once inside them, but on their edges they are confusing. . . . Biology has a word for these blurred edges: *ecotone.*" An ecotone is in No One's Land; it

> is the margin between habitats—the zone in which the treeline is a segueway where high-altitude, stunted pines grow among lowland red maples; where the ground is soggy but shows little other evidence of swampy muck ahead; where a mysterious eight-foot green wall of leaves and saplings forms a curtain between an airy meadow and the silent gloom of a pine wood.
>
> An ecotone is an environment at a boundary. . . . natural boundaries are not sharp edges, but are unique, synergistic combinations of their adjacent habitats, containing their own unique biota. Chestnut-sided warblers, for example, are almost exclusively creatures of the edges of the meadow. . . . With habitats one finds orderliness in the stable center of a place, by identifying common denominators. With ecotones one focuses on the dynamic disorderliness of unstable edges . . .

Ecotones, with their uniquely synergistic combinations and unstable edges, are the natural analogue—perhaps the precursors—of the persona, that "system of relationships," in Jung's words, "whereby I am never apart from the effect of the object on me." Places are never apart from each other's effects, and depend on these effects for their own realization. Remember the mountain looking into my window, its features more sharply defined by that unstable meteorological boundary known as a frontal system that brought from ocean the season's first snow. And the memorable trees that provided a meeting-place for Les and I at the edge of the Russian river. Here too are ecotones, personae. The persona as ecotone is no one-sided or Janus-faced mask, but a multidirectional system of faces at once unique and infinitely—dramatically—various. The ecotone as persona signifies the empathetic relatedness of places, the place where differences can meet. The place where places can meet, not in stable states of identity, of polarized opposition, or of fusion and merger, but in ecstatic exchanges of idiosyncrasies, in states of fecund marginalization. Asano Park is an ecotone.

Ecotones are also the means by which qualities (spirits) of distinct habitats migrate among each other. It is telling that, when Sauer's mind wanders from the arbitrary grid, its first move is "to reconstruct the flight paths of . . . monarchs" migrating southward in the early fall. This is a revealing move; the monarch butterflies—butterflies being images of the psyche—are creatures of ecotones, entomological personae signifying the migrating powers of places. And the powers of places have their own migratory patterns. Asano Park migrates to myriad places where trees and vegetation are commemoratively planted, as did the first atomic bombings to South Floridian memories after Hurricane Andrew.

Asano Park signifies not only, and not primarily, the search for a certain kind of normality and security, but, more importantly, a deeper forgetting of the same. What abides is a defined sense of place—a particularity that infuses but cannot ultimately be reduced to a group's self-definition. Asano Park must somehow remember the *kami* or sacred presence which, in ancient Japanese myth, first takes up residence in the place where trees grow thick. That treed sense of sacredness cannot be confined to any group, however; it has kin in numberless religious cosmologies. It cannot be confined to the human sphere either, but is at the same time an experience of wild otherness—the uncanny, the inhuman. Thus, if we go deeply enough into the spirit of a place, the very normalcy and security associated with it are undermined, and we find ourselves in the presence of the extraordinary, the uncannily powerful (this also is an intention of Zen-garden ecology, its art of memory). The familiar shows its foreign face.

> *Speaking in my place is someone not human—the dead son of the Hiroshima father who wears the rabbi's prayer shawl. He has been speaking all along and I didn't realize that my words were also his. I thought I was remembering land but it turns out to have been him. I begin to understand the need to give his words their place, to identify in my practice, my writing, the ghost of his religious longing.*
>
> *And his words speak in turn for multitudes of others: dead daughters and sons, their memories crying for water, strewn in fields of boulders blasted into place by the volcano that borders the decimated land. Rocks whose shapes remember their histories. Deforested lands whose lives bleed into seas. Silenced languages of the extinct—frogs, birds, trees, others. Cries of those who follow.*
>
> *All theirs is the speaking for which the sadness of Hiroshima forever prays.*

In Hiroshima, in imagination's Asano Park, in the Place of All Souls, we glimpse how the cross-cutting work of ecological protection and restoration leads toward the death of identity's ideology of apartness, and how the ecology of identification fosters more explicit "ecological identification" and, ultimately, celebratory love of the world.[17] And how this larger and commemorative identification involves a certain forgetting, a letting-go of self. Plant ecologist

Barbara McClintock, reflecting on her friendship with the constitu-
ents of plants' and animals' lives, the chromosomes, shows us a
way: "I actually felt as if I was right down there [with chromosomes under the microscope] and these were my friends . . . As you
look at these things, they become part of you. And you forget
yourself."[18] We are all down there, under a microscope, a delimited
and concentrated place that is yet a whole world the place of whose
time is after Hiroshima. The things upon which the narrative of
Hiroshima focuses become part of us, and we become part of them.

Placed under the microscope of Hiroshima, we become more
able to identify and discriminate with rather than against others,
and our imaginations of boundaries themselves become more
discriminating. This, in turn, can help mobilize concern with a
crucial ecological need—protecting and restoring ecosystem
integrity, which means remembering also the fluid, porous, and
unique characteristics of the places where ecosystems meet. Our
place-making energies move from preoccupations with national
(military) defense—and defense of identity—to ecosystem protection,
to cognizant empathy for the roles of ecotones. We more deeply
sense how No One's Land remembers. In this remembrance, love
of the natural world combines with a mournful recognition of our
species' deep-rooted woundedness, and of what we have inflicted on
the land. We deepen our capacity for conversation with the planet's
other powers, begin to think like them. Love like them.

Asano Park locates the post-Hiroshima ecology of place. Our
ecology of place. Think like it. Remember with Father Kleinsorge
"the silence in the grove by the river, where hundreds of grue-
somely wounded suffered together"—"one of the most dreadful and
awesome phenomena of his whole experience"—and the trees: those
whose morning shelter fell to the searing whirlwind of the bomb's
first afternoon.[19] Think like Asano Park—its awful silence, its trees
of decimation, its rivers of bodies, its injured remembering
chromosomes.

Like the ancient longings—familiar and foreign, humane but not
necessarily human or consoling—also in its memory. Like Father

Kleinsorge himself. For he is the foreigner (p. 6) whose wounds are opened by the "stranger," the Japanese woman, who offers him tea leaves for his thirst. Remember her "gentleness" that "made [him] suddenly want to cry," so great was the contrast between her kindness and "the hatred of foreigners" that so troubled him. This gentle offering of leaves, this depth of desire, thinks like the place. It allows constrictive identities to be forgotten, to die, to finally be placed aboard the ferries of lamentation, to become shades, personae, for the rivers of lands, of memories, of care. Thinking like Asano Park means to suffer together the ecology of mourning, to commemorate together the reforesting of hospitality—the meeting-place of all places, the place of all souls.

Hiroshima touches, with his raw hand, the rough charred cheek of Who-on-Earth, whose smile remains faint yet striking—distinct, enigmatic. The friction abruptly reminds him of his wounds, but he is reminded of something else too. He remembers, in that touch, the impression of the rough-barked maple under which he used to sit, facing the river. That place is separated from him by caverns far above. Yet he will remember the tree always, for its spirit will flourish in the lobed leaves of his unhealed hands.

Notes

CHAPTER 1

1. John Hersey, *Hiroshima* (New York: Bantam Books, 1985, rev. ed.), p. 152.

2. Quoted in Jeff Jacoby, "Smithsonian still doesn't get it," *The Boston Globe*, Jan. 1995.

3. Kai Bird, "The Curators Cave In," op-ed article, *The New York Times*, 9 October 1994, p. A19.

4. Nelson Mandela, *Long Walk to Freedom: The Autobiography of Nelson Mandela* (Boston/New York: Little, Brown and Co., 1994), p. 544.

5. Hersey, *Hiroshima*, p. 53.

6. Peter Bishop, *The Greening of Psychology: The Vegetable World in Myth, Dream, and Healing* (Dallas, TX: Spring Publications, Inc., 1990), p. 3.

7. Robert Jay Lifton, *Death in Life: Survivors of Hiroshima* (Chapel Hill: University of North Carolina Press, 1991 [1969]), p. 68.

8. Spencer Weart, *Nuclear Fear: A History of Images* (Cambridge: Harvard

University Press, 1988), p. 325.

9. Brent Staples, *Parallel Time: Growing Up in Black and White* (New York: Pantheon Books, 1994), p. 255.

10. See my *Imaginal Memory and the Place of Hiroshima* (Albany: State University of New York Press, 1988).

11. "Secret cargo called top Russia air defense," quoted in *The Boston Globe*, 25 December 1994, 15.

12. Robert Lowell, "Fall 1961" in *For the Union Dead* (New York: Farrar, Strauss & Giroux, 1965), p. 11.

13. An exception has been Princeton scholar Stephen Cohen, who since the collapse of the Soviet Union has consistently criticized the missionary self-righteousness of American policies toward Russia.

14. Ervin Staub, *The Roots of Evil: The Origins of Genocide and Other Group Violence* (Cambridge: Cambridge University Press, 1989), p. 58.

15. "Too Many Nuclear Labs," *New York Times* editorial of 26 August, p. A28.

16. See Robert Jay Lifton, *The Protean Self: Human Resilience in an Age of Fragmentation* (New York: Basic Books, 1993).

17. Cornel West, *Race Matters* (Boston: Beacon Press, 1993).

18. Browne, Malcolm W., "Most precise gauge yet points to global warming: satellite data indicate seas' levels are rising around the world," *The New York Times*, 20 December 1994, p. C4; Dean Roemmich and John McGowan, "Climatic Warming and the Decline of Zooplankton," *Science* 3 March 1995, v. 267: 1324–26; "Early Warning? Resurgence in infectious diseases linked to warming planet, Harvard scientists say," *The Boston Globe*, 6 March 95, pp. 25, 28; "Global Warming Resumed in 1994, Climate Data Show," *The New York Times*, 27 January 1995, pp. A1, A13. Article on El Niño cited in following paragraph is titled "El Niño Is Doing It Again: Stormy West, Balmy East," *The New York Times*, 14 January 1995, p. A1; op-ed piece quoted is by D. James

Baker, "When the Rains Came," *The Washington Post*, 25 January 1995, p. A25. I am indebted to Gar Smith of Earth Island Institute for his comments on the inadequacy of the term "global warming" as a descriptor for the uneven effects of an overall rise in the planet's temperature.

19. *The Challenge of Peace: God's Promise and Our Response*, par. 302; in *Catholics and Nuclear War*, ed. Philip J. Murnion (New York: Crossroad Publishing Co., 1983), p. 329.

20. Eqbal Amhad, Presentation on Hindu and Muslim Fundamentalism, Center on Violence and Human Survival, City University of New York, 1990.

21. Donald M. Murray, "The rosy past that never was," *The Boston Globe*, 6 December 1994, p. 42.

CHAPTER 2

1. *Republic*, 621A.

2. Nelson Mandela, *Long Walk to Freedom: The Autobiography of Nelson Mandela* (Boston/New York: Little, Brown and Co., 1994), pp. 96, 97.

3. Robert D. Kaplan, *Balkan Ghosts: A Journey Through History* (New York: Random House, 1993), p. 152.

4. The paucity of timely contemplation by social scientists and others on post-Cold War psychological challenges in international relations is especially remarkable given the many volumes written on the psychology of international and intergroup relations in the past few decades, and especially during the surge of nuclear fear in the 1980's.

5. See Edward Casey, *Getting Back into Place: Toward a Renewed Understanding of the Place-World* (Bloomington: Indiana University Press, 1993), pp. 48–49.

6. James Hersh discusses this matter perceptively in his work-in-progress, *Blinding the Cyclops: Thinking the End of Racism*.

7. I am indebted to psychoanalyst Edward Emery for sharing in conversation his research and insights into the depths and nuances of the mourning process.

8. John E. Mack, "Nationalism and the Self," *The Psychohistory Review*, 11, 2–3 (1983): 60.

9. Jean Bethke Elshtain, *Democracy on Trial* (New York: Basic Books, 1995). See especially pp. 42–58 on the ideology of victimization and "progressive" identity politics, and chapter 3, "The Politics of Difference."

CHAPTER 3

1. Frances Yates, *The Art of Memory* (Chicago: University of Chicago Press, 1966), p. 10.

2. See James Hillman, *Re-Visioning Psychology* (New York: Harper & Row, 1975), ch. 2.

3. Edward Casey, *Getting Back into Place: Toward a Renewed Understanding of the Place-World* (Bloomington: Indiana University Press, 1993), pp. 151, 152.

4. See C. T. Onions, ed., *The Oxford Dictionary of English Etymology* (Oxford: Oxford University Press, 1966), p. 194. Quoted in Edward S. Casey, *Remembering: A Phenomenological Study* (Bloomington: Indiana University Press, 1987), p. 217; on "intrapsychic memorialization," see pp. 239–43. I am indebted to Casey's exploration of commemoration (ibid., chapter 10), which helped me better understand what Hiroshima asks of us.

5. Maurice Halbwachs, *The Collective Memory*, tr. Francis J. Ditter and Vida Yazdi Ditter (Harper & Row, Inc., 1980 [1950]), p. 23; italics added.

6. Brent Staples, *Parallel Time: Growing Up in Black and White* (New York: Pantheon Books, 1994), pp. 3, 4, 8; quotes in following paragraph from pp. 9–11.

7. John M. Broughton and Marta Zahayevich, "The Peace Movement Threat" in *Education for a Living World*, ed. Douglas Sloan (New York: Teachers College Press, 1983), pp. 153, 152.

8.   Gaston Bachelard, *The Poetics of Space*, tr. Etienne Gilson (Boston: Beacon Press, 1966), p. xxxiii; italics in original. Following quotes from pp. 8, 13, 56.

9.   Sigmund Freud, *The Interpretation of Dreams*, trans. and ed. James Strachey (New York: Avon Books, 1965), pp. 564, 139 n.

10. Loren Eiseley, *The Invisible Pyramid* (New York: Charles Scribner's Sons, 1970), pp. 2–3.

11. Bachelard, *Poetics*, p. 4.

12. Marsilio Ficino, *The Book of Life [De vita triplici]*, tr. Charles Boer (Irving, Texas: Spring Publications, Inc., 1980), ch. 19.

CHAPTER 4

1.   See Cicero, *De oratore* II. lxxvi. 351–4. Further references to the *De oratore* follow the Loeb classics edition, tr. E. W. Sutton and H. Rackham (Cambridge: Harvard University Press, 1948), with book and section numbers indicated in the text. For further information on this story see Frances Yates, *The Art of Memory* (Chicago: University of Chicago Press, 1966), p. 10.pp. 1–2 and 27–9; also Quintilian, *Institutio oratoria* XI. ii. 11–6, for a critical account of different versions of the story.

2.   *Ad Herennium libri VI* (III. xvi. 28–xxiv. 40), probably written around 86–82 B.C.E. The version of *Ad Herennium* followed here is translated by Harry Caplan (New York: Loeb Classical Library, 1968), modified in some instances following Yates.

3.   Ibid, III. xxii. 37.

4.   Yates, *Art of Memory*, p. 10.

5.   James Hillman, *The Myth of Analysis* (New York: Harper & Row, 1978 [1972]), p. 199.

6.   On p. 174 of John Ciardi's translation and edition of Dante Aligheri, *The Inferno* (New York: The New American Library, Inc., 1954.

7. Yates, *Art of Memory*, p. 104.

8. James Hillman, *Re-Visioning Psychology* (New York: Harper & Row, 1975), p. 95.

9. On the archetypal imagery of Priapus, see Lopez-Pedraza, *Hermes and His Children* (Irving, Texas: Spring Publications, 1977), ch. 6.

10. Alphonso Lingis, *The Community of Those Who have Nothing in Common*, (Bloomington: Indiana University Press, 1994), pp. 30–31.

11. John Hersey, *Hiroshima* (New York: Bantam Books, 1985, rev. ed.), pp. 1–2.

12. Gaston Bachelard, *The Poetics of Space*, tr. Etienne Gilson (Boston: Beacon Press, 1966), p. 9.

13. In *Re-Visioning Psychology*, p. 94.

14. Hersey, *Hiroshima*, p. 3.

15. Ibid., p. 48.

16. Ibid., p. 58.

17. For comparative material see Mircea Eliade, *Shamanism*, tr. Willard R. Trask (New York: Bollingen Foundation, 1964), pp. 355ff, 361 and 417; Arnold Van Gennep, *The Rites of Passage* tr. Monika B. Vizedom and Gabrielle L. Caffee (Chicago: The University of Chicago Press, 1960), pp. 153, 54, 57.

18. *Inferno* III. 79.

19. Paul Boyer documents initial American reaction to the atomic bombings in *By the Bomb's Early Light: American Thought and Culture at the Dawn of the Atomic Age* (New York: Pantheon, 1985), esp. ch. 1.

20. Quoted in Raymond Klibansky, Erwin Panofsky and Fritz Saxl, *Saturn and Melancholy* (London: Nelson, 1964), p. 258.

21. See ibid., pp. 69–72.

22. *Ad Herennium libri VI*, (III. xvi. 28–xxiv. 40), translated by Harry Caplan (New York: Loeb Classical Library, 1968), III. xix. 31.

23. See Sigmund Freud, "Mourning and Melancholia," trans. under the supervision of Joan Riviere, Collected Papers, vol. 4 (New York: Basic Books, 1969).

24. Yates, *Art of Memory,* p. 8.

CHAPTER 5

1. C. G. Jung, *Memories, Dreams, Reflections*, trans. Richard and Clara Winston (New York: Vintage Books, 1965), pp. 175, 181, 191.

2. For more detailed accounts of active imagination see Jung, *Analytical Psychology: Its Theory & Practice* (New York: Vintage Books, 1970), pp. 190–204; Mary Watkins, *Waking Dreams* (New York: Harper & Row, 1977 [1976]), pp. 42–51; Janet Dallett, "Active Imagination in Practice" in *Jungian Analysis*, ed. Murray Stein (La Salle, IL: Open Court Publishing Co., 1982), pp. 172–91 and references.

3. Edward S. Casey, *Remembering: A Phenomenological Study* (Bloomington: Indiana University Press, 1987), pp. 274–5. See Freud's Letter of December 1, 1896 [to Wilhelm Fliess] in *The Standard Edition of the Complete Psychological Works of Sigmund Freud* (London: Hogarth, 1953–74), 1: 233.

4. Casey, *Remembering*, pp. 242, 239–43, 247.

5. Edward Emery, personal communication. Edward Casey, in his more recent work on the power of place, also speaks of implacement (or "placialization"), focusing on the ways in which one inevitably comes to dwell in—to be shaped by and to shape—particular, actual places. See *Getting Back into Place: Toward a Renewed Understanding of the Place-World* (Bloomington: Indiana University Press, 1993), ch. 1.

CHAPTER 6

1. Quoted in Yasuhiko Taketomo, "Hiroshima and Denial," in *Psychoanalysis and the Nuclear Threat: Clinical and Theoretical Studies*, ed. Howard B. Levine, Daniel Jacobs, and Lowell J. Rubin (New York: The Analytic Press, 1988), p. 259.

2. Edward S. Casey, "Getting Placed: Soul in Space," *Spring 1982*: 9–10.

3. Floyd Hiatt Ross, *Shinto: The Way of Japan* (Boston: Beacon Press, 1965), p. 64.

4. See my *The Power of Trees: The Reforesting of the Soul* (Dallas: Spring Publications, 1994), p. 96

5. Edward Casey, "Getting Placed," p. 7.

6. For a popular account of differing views on whether to include Kyoto on the list of atomic-bomb targets, see Peter Wyden (*Day One: Before Hiroshima and After* [New York: Warner Books, 1985]), pp. 191–198.

7. This and following two quotes from Alexander H. Deighton, *Human Relations in a Changing World: Observations on the Use of the Social Sciences* (New York: E. P. Dutton & Co., Inc., 1949), p. 21.

8. Ibid., p. 35.

9. Casey, "Getting Placed," pp. 16–7.

10. Quoted by Robert Sardello in "City as Metaphor, City as Mystery," *Spring 1982*: 97.

11. Casey, "Getting Placed," p. 16.

12. John Hersey, *Hiroshima* (New York: Bantam Books, 1985, rev. ed.), p. 86.

13. Quoted in Robert Jay Lifton, *Death in Life: Survivors of Hiroshima* (Chapel Hill: University of North Carolina Press, 1991 [1969]), p. 86.

14. See Kai Erikson's *A New Species of Trouble* (New York: W.W. Norton & Co., 1994), p. 240.

15. *Hiroshima*, p. 76.

16. As Edward Casey points out, even a linear conception of time presupposes a sequence of place-structures (*Getting Back into Place: Toward a Renewed Understanding of the Place-World* [Bloomington: Indiana University Press, 1993], pp. 9–13). Moreover, "There is *no (grasping of) time without place;* and this is so precisely by virtue of place's actively delimiting and creatively conditioning capacities" (p. 21).

17. Deighton, *Human Relations*, p. 20. Following quotes from p. 21.

18. Ibid., p. 38.

19. Jonathan Schell, *The Fate of the Earth* (New York: Alfred A. Knopf, 1982), pp. 46–7.

20. Mircea Eliade, *The Sacred and the Profane*, tr. Willard R. Trask (New York: Harcourt, Brace & World, 1959), ch. 2.

21. Printed in *The Amicus Journal* (Spring 1985): 40.

22. Implicit in this discussion is the idea that time can be "timeless," but *not* placeless—since time presupposes place. This means that timelessness always has some place, some location, even if only an abstract one. Says Casey, "time is a place" (*Getting Back,* p. 20)—so too timelessness.

CHAPTER 7

1. Following quotes from Sir James Frazer are from *The New Golden Bough*, rev. and ed. Theodor H. Gaster (New York: S. G. Phillips, 1959), pp. 718, 720.

2. *Hiroshima and Nagasaki: The Physical, Medical and Social Effects of the Atomic Bombings*, ed. The Committee for the Compilation of Materials on Damage Caused by the Atomic Bombs in Hiroshima and Nagasaki, tr. Eisei

Tshikawa and David L. Swain (New York: Basic Books, Inc., 1981), pp. 484–5.

3. Robert Jay Lifton, *Death in Life: Survivors of Hiroshima*, (Chapel Hill: University of North Carolina Press, 1991 [1969]), pp. 9–10.

4. Masuji Ibuse, *Black Rain*, tr. John Bester (Tokyo and Palo Alto: Kodansha International, Ltd., 1969), p. 92.

5. Robert Jungk, *Children of the Ashes* (New York: Harcourt, Brace & World, 1961), p. 184.

6. Arata Osada, Ph.D., comp., *Children of Hiroshima*, tr. not given (New York: Harper & Row, 1982 [1951]), p. 166.

7. Ibid., p. 213.

8. *Unforgettable Fire: Pictures Drawn by Atomic Bomb Survivors*, ed. Japan Broadcasting Corporation [NHK] (New York: Pantheon Books, 1977), pp. 52-3

9. Ibid., p. 68.

10. Takashi Nagai, *We of Nagasaki* (New York: Duell, Sloan and Pearce, 1951), p. 189.

11. John Hersey, *Hiroshima* (New York: Bantam Books, 1985, rev. ed.), p. 87.

12. The 3rd-century alchemist, Zosimos, records for us a vision of the un-healing wounds of alchemy. See C. G. Jung, "The Visions of Zosimos," *Alchemical Studies, Collected Works*, Volume 13, trans. R. F. C. Hull (Princeton: Princeton University Press, Bollingen Series XX, 1976), par. 86).

CHAPTER 8

1. Following are some of the notable accounts of the bombings of Hiroshima and Nagasaki that the reader may wish to consult. The most through account of the effects of the atomic bombings is: *Hiroshima and Nagasaki: The Physical, Medical and Social Effects of the Atomic Bombings*, ed. The Committee

for the Compilation of Materials on Damage Caused by the Atomic Bombs in Hiroshima and Nagasaki, tr. Eisei Tshikawa and David L. Swain (New York: Basic Books, Inc., 1981). Testimonies of *hibakusha* include: Arata Osada, Ph.D., comp., *Children of Hiroshima*, tr. not given (New York: Harper & Row, 1982 [1951]) — a collection of short essays by *hibakusha* who were children at the time of the bombing; Michihiko Hachiya, M.D., *Hiroshima Diary*, ed. and tr. Warner Wells, M.D. (Chapel Hill: The University of North Carolina Press, 1955); Takashi Nagai, *We of Nagasaki* (New York: Duell, Sloan and Pearce, 1951); Hiroshima-Nagasaki Publishing Committee, *Days to Remember: An Account of the Bombings of Hiroshima and Nagasaki* (Tokyo: Hiroshima-Nagasaki Publishing Comm., 1981) — a photographic record of the bombings; and *Unforgettable Fire: Pictures Drawn by Atomic Bomb Survivors*, ed. Japan Broadcasting Corporation [NHK] (New York: Pantheon Books, 1977), with images that many find to be among the most powerful renderings of the atomic-bomb experience. The classic novelistic account of the bombing of Hiroshima (by a non*hibakusha*) is Masuji Ibuse's *Black Rain*, tr. John Bester (Tokyo and Palo Alto: Kodansha International, Ltd., 1969). A good collection of short stories, most of which are written by *hibakusha*, is in Kenzaburo Oe, ed., *The Crazy Iris and other Stories of the Atomic Aftermath* (New York: Grove Press, Inc., 1985). See also Robert Jungk, *Children of the Ashes* (New York: Harcourt, Brace & World, 1961), for a sensitive account of the severe guilt and other sufferings of *hibakusha*, and of the struggles around the rebuilding of Hiroshima. Millen Brand, in *Peace March: Nagasaki to Hiroshima* (Woodstock, VT: The Countryman Press, Inc., 1980) combines lyric and documentary elements in an account of his 1977 trip to Nagasaki and Hiroshima during which he joined with the Japanese for anniversary commemorations of the bombings.

2.   Robert Jay Lifton (*Death in Life: Survivors of Hiroshima* [Chapel Hill: University of North Carolina Press, 1969 (1991)], pp. 19–30), speaks of an overwhelming "immersion" in death.

3.   Robert Lowell, "For the Union Dead," *For the Union Dead* (New York: Farrar, Strauss, & Giroux, 1965), p. 72.

4.   Edward S. Casey, *Getting Back into Place: Toward a Renewed Understanding of the Place-World* (Bloomington: Indiana University Press, 1993), p. x.

5.   John Hersey, *Hiroshima* (New York: Bantam Books, 1985, rev. ed.), p. 25.

The following quotes are from pp. 45, 46, 48.

CHAPTER 9

1. John Hersey, *Hiroshima* (New York: Knopf, 1985, rev. ed.), p. 63.

2. Michihiko Hachiya, M.D., *Hiroshima Diary*, tr. and ed. Warner Wells, M.D. (Chapel Hill: The University of North Carolina press, 1955), pp. 15–6.

3. Masuji Ibuse, *Black Rain*, tr. John Bester (Tokyo and Palo Alto: Kodansha International, Ltd., 1969), p. 159.

4. Robert Jay Lifton, *Death in Life: Survivors of Hiroshima* (Chapel Hill: University of North Carolina Press, 1991), p. 51.

5. Ibid., p. 489; italics in original.

6. Quoted in ibid., p. 36.

7. Hachiya, *Hiroshima Diary*, p. 101.

8. Ibid., pp. 114–5.

9. Richard Rhodes, *The Making of the Atomic Bomb* (New York: Simon & Schuster, 1986), p. 747.

10. A good account of the religious background of Japanese nationalism and associated politics is Joseph M. Kitagawa's *Religion in Japanese History* (New York: Columbia University Press, 1966).

11. Quoted in C. G. Jung, *Mysterium Coniunctionis, Collected Works*, Volume 14, trans. R. F. C. Hull (Princeton: Princeton University Press, Bollingen Series XX, 1963), par. 46; previous quote from par. 45.

12. Marsilio Ficino, *The Book of Life*, tr. Charles Boer (Irving, TX: Spring Publications, Inc., 1980), ch. 11.

CHAPTER 10

1.   See my *The Power of Trees: The Reforesting of the Soul* (Dallas: Spring Publications, 1994).

2.   John Hersey, *Hiroshima* (New York: Alfred A. Knopf, 1985, rev. ed.), p. 35.

3.   Alexander H. Deighton, *Human Relations in a Changing World: Observations on the Use of the Social Sciences* (New York: E. P. Dutton & Co., Inc., 1949), p. 29.

4.   Tatsuichiro Akizuki, *Nagasaki 1945*, trans. Keiichi Nagata and ed. Gordon Honeycombe (London: Quartet Books, 1981), pp. 36, 37.

5.   Catherine S. Manegold, "Alien Terrain Replaces What Was Once Home," *The New York Times*, Monday, August 31, 1992, p. A1.

6.   For examples, see my *The Power of Trees: The Reforesting of the Soul* (Dallas: Spring Publications, 1994), ch. 6.

7.   Michael Dillon, "Reborn from Holocaust," *The Geographical Magazine*: 402.

8.   Robert D. Kaplan, *Balkan Ghosts: A Journey Through History* (New York: Random House, 1993), p. 188.

9.   Y. Ota, quoted in Robert Jay Lifton, "The Image of 'The End of the World," in *Facing Apocalypse*, ed. Valerie Andrews et al. (Dallas, Texas: Spring Publications, Inc., 1987), p. 28.

CHAPTER 11

1.   Nelson Mandela, *Long Walk to Freedom: The Autobiography of Nelson Mandela* (Boston/New York: Little, Brown and Company, 1994), p. 200. The following quotes are from pp. 106, 110, 116.

2.   See Neil Evernden, *The Social Creation of Nature* (Baltimore: The John

Hopkins University Press, 1992), pp. 116, 132–33.

3. John Keats, *Letter to Richard Woodhouse,* 27 October 1818; in *English Romantic Writers,* ed. David Perkins (New York: Harcourt Brace Jovanovich, Inc., 1967), p. 1220.

4. Erik H. Erikson, *Childhood and Society* (New York: W. W. Norton & Co., 1963, rev. ed.), p. 261.

5. C. G. Jung, *Two Essays on Analytical Psychology,* trans. R. F. C. Hull (Princeton: Princeton University Press, Bollingen Series XX, 1977, rev. ed.), pp. 192, 193.

6. C. G. Jung, *Analytical Psychology: Notes of the Seminar Given in 1925,* edited by William McGuire (Princeton: Princeton University Press, Bollingen Series XCIX, 1989), pp. 108–09.

7. Walt Whitman, "Song of Myself," 1324–26.

8. Robert Jay Lifton, *The Protean Self: Human Resilience in an Age of Fragmentation* (New York: Basic Books, 1993). On the importance of "cross-cutting relations," see Ervin Staub, *The Roots of Evil: The Origins of Genocide and Other Group Violence* (Cambridge: Cambridge University Press, 1989), pp. 274–76, 278–79. I prefer the phrase "cross-cutting connections" because it evokes the paradox of mourning—something must be *cut,* wounded, in order for deeper *connection* to take place.

9. Cornel West, *Race Matters* (Boston: Beacon Press, 1993), p. 150.

10. Personal communication, 18 January 1995.

CHAPTER 12

1. Robert D. Kaplan, *Balkan Ghosts: A Journey Through History* (New York: Random House, 1993), p. 59.

2. See Aldo Leopold, *A Sand Country Almanac: With Essays from Round River* (New York: Ballantine Books, 1990 [1966]), pp 137–41. The following

quotes, from his "In Defense of the Land Ethic," are from pp. 216 and 253, respectively.

3. Ibid., p. 241.

4. Catherine L. Albanese, *Nature Religion in America: From the Algonkian Indians to the New Age* (Chicago/London: University of Chicago Press, 1990), p. 75.

5. James Hillman, *The Myth of Analysis* (New York: Harper & Row, 1978 [1972]), p. 179.

6. Sigmund Freud, *New Introductory Lectures on Psychoanalysis*, tr. James Strachey (New York: W. W. Norton & Co., Inc., 1964), p. 105.

7. The term is E. V. Walter's. See his article on "The Places of Experience," *The Philosophical Forum*, XII, 2 (1980–1), and his book *Placeways: A Theory of the Human Environment* (Chapel Hill: University of North Carolina Press, 1988.

8. James Oglivy, *Many Dimensional Man: Decentralizing Self, Society and the Sacred* (New York: Harper & Row, 1979 [1977]), pp. 124–5

9. Jacques Derrida, *The Other Heading: Reflections on Today's Europe*, trans. Pascale-Anne Brault and Michael B. Naas (Bloomington & Indianapolis: Indiana University Press, 1992), pp. 42, 39.

10. Edward S. Casey, "Getting Placed: Soul in Space," *Spring 1982*: 4. See also Casey's *Getting Back into Place* (Bloomington: Indiana University Press, 1993), pp. 6–12.

11. Tr. J. Veitch in *The Rationalists* (Garden City: Doubleday, 1960), p. 63; quoted in Joel Kovel, *Against the State of Nuclear Terror* (Boston: South End Press, 1984, rev. ed.), p. 123.

12. Casey, *Getting Back into Place: Toward a Renewed Understanding of the Place-World* (Bloomington: Indiana University Press, 1993), p. 15.

13. Ibid., p. 111.

14. E. V. Walter, "Places," p. 172.

15. Michael Dillon, "Reborn from Holocaust," *The Geographical Magazine*: 402.

16. Peter Sauer, "Ecotones," *Orion*, Winter 1995: 60, 61.

17. See, for example, the discussions of identification in Warwick Fox, *Toward a Transpersonal Ecology: Developing New Foundations for Environmentalism* (Boston: Shambhala, 1990), pp. 229–233 and ch. 8; Joanna Macy's moving volume on *Self as Lover, Self as World* (Philadelphia: New Society Publishers, 1993); and Andrew McLaughlin, *Regarding Nature: Industrialism and Deep Ecology* (Albany, NY: State University of New York Press, 1993), pp. 187–88, 194–95, and 207–08.

18. Quoted in Evelyn Fox Keller, "Women and Basic Research: Respecting the Unexpected," *Technology Review*, Nov./Dec. 1984: 46.

19. Hersey, *Hiroshima* (New York: Alfred A. Knopf, 1985, rev. ed.), p. 36. Following quote from p. 53.

Index

Credits